SPIRITUALLY WOUNDED WARRIORS:
AN ARMY OF ONE ANOTHER

Spiritually Wounded Warriors: An Army of One Another
Edward L. Linebaugh, U.S. Army (Retired)
Publisher/General Editor/Contributing Author

Copyright © 2022

All rights reserved. No part of this book may be used or reproduced by any means without the publisher's written permission except in the case of brief quotations citing the editor and author.

Except where noted, Scripture quotations are from The ESV® Bible (The Holy Bible, English Standard Version®), copyright © 2001 by Crossway, a publishing ministry of Good News Publishers. Used by permission. All rights reserved.

Cover Design by Michael Advertising Group, Huntsville, AL
Used by permission.

Printed in the United States of America

InLine Publishers, LLC
P.O. Box 12793
Huntsville, AL 35815

Image used in the page headers:
U.S. Army Combat Medical Badge

DEDICATION

This military ministry manual is dedicated in

memory of our beloved battle brother,

Joe Bryant, U.S. Air Force veteran, and contributing author

of *Spiritual Battle Rattle: God's Armor,*

Military Veterans' Review of Ephesians 6:10-18,

who valiantly fought against the

spiritual forces of evil and has attained

spiritual Victory in Jesus (V-J Day) and

is at eternal rest with God's faithful soldiers.

ACKNOWLEDGEMENTS

First and most notably, I thank our heavenly Father for His beloved Son, our Lord Jesus Christ, and the Holy Spirit for healing my intermittent spiritual battle injuries. To my loving and gracious wife, Kathy, for her patience and godly example throughout our 45 years of marriage. Thank you for standing with me! I am also grateful and indebted to our children, Nicole, and Paul, for their resilience as military kids—*Army brats*—and for keeping the faith and their spiritual growth. "I pray that you may prosper in every way and be in good health physically just as you are spiritually" (3 John 2, HCSB).

I am also greatly appreciative of our spiritual/church family from Bremerhaven, Germany, in the late 1980s with whom we spent several wonderful, life-changing years together: Darren and Jennifer, Ann, Tim, Jon and Sherri, Louis and Venus, Anthony and Karen, Kevin and Cindy, Robin and Donna Marie, Joe and Karen, Dave and Maxine and many others whom I do not recall—God knows who you are. *Stay Spiritually Strong*!

Spiritually Wounded Warriors: An Army of One Another

TABLE OF CONTENTS

FORWARD	
PROLOGUE	
CHAPTER 1	Spiritual Battle Buddies
CHAPTER 2	Spiritual Battle Wounds: WIA, KIA, & MIA
CHAPTER 3	Spiritual Suicide
CHAPTER 4	Spiritual Friendly Fire & High-Risk Behaviors
CHAPTER 5	Spiritual Combat Casualty Care: Bloody Bunny
CHAPTER 6	Spiritual Echelons of Care
CHAPTER 7	Spiritual Battle Scars
CHAPTER 8	Spiritual Medicine & Treatment Plans
CHAPTER 9	Spiritual Recovery
CHAPTER 10	Spiritual V-J Day
EPILOGUE	The Sum of All Tears
APPENDIX A	Military Jargon / Acronyms
APPENDIX B	Bible Translations / Versions

FORWARD

Ranger School is one of the most challenging institutes the U.S. military offers. It is physically demanding and mentally draining. Lack of sleep and food tax the students, and extreme pressure makes for an almost unbearable situation if attempted alone. The school cadre realizes this and assigns each student a Ranger buddy. You go everywhere with them. You run, hike, dig foxholes, eat, and march with your Ranger buddy. They are your advocate to tough it out, as you are his or hers. Unsurprisingly, the concept of a Ranger buddy is biblical. Ecclesiastes 4:9-12 states,

> Two are better than one, because they have a good reward for their toil. For if they fall, one will lift up his fellow. But woe to him who is alone when he falls and has not another to lift him up! Again, if two lie together, they keep warm, but how can one keep warm alone? And though a man might prevail against one who is alone, two will withstand him—a threefold cord is not quickly broken.

Jesus understood the power of a spiritual Ranger buddy when he sent out the apostles two by two (Mark 6:7). We all need a spiritual Ranger buddy; do you have one? I do and have had the same one for over 30 years. Let me explain.

I was a young Army Captain commanding an Infantry company stationed in Germany. We deployed for Operation Desert Storm, where my company was literally at the spear's tip for the entire ground war. It was a short but extremely violent battle for my unit. After the war, I returned to Germany and then to the United States. While I do not know if I could be diagnosed with post-traumatic stress disorder, I know something was wrong with me. I seemed to be in a fog, unmotivated and engaging in self-defeating behavior. I did not know where to turn or to whom. You see, I was not a Christian. Then I met someone who would become my spiritual Ranger buddy who introduced me to Jesus Christ. It was like the fog lifted upon being baptized, and I was relieved. My spiritual Ranger buddy indeed helped me to overcome what were mental and spiritual wounds. We are still there for each other because I *married her thirty years ago.*

Our worst enemy, Satan, "prowls around like a roaring lion, seeking someone to devour" (1 Peter 5:8) and always seeks to wound or kill us spiritually. We need to band together to defeat him. This book, *Spiritually Wounded Warriors: An Army of One Another*, lays out the strategy and battle plan for doing so. It shows no weakness in leaning on one another. Instead, it reveals that we understand the Bible's tenets that prove that two (or more) are better than one in spiritual warfare.

Ed Linebaugh, a fellow retired soldier, enlisted a spiritual Ranger squad of veterans from multiple walks of life with varied experiences and education to address our need to rely on each other and bear one another's burdens (Galatians 6:2). Be blessed!

TONY TURNER, Lieutenant Colonel, U.S. Army, Retired
MOS: Infantry
Knoxville, Tennessee
EMAIL: turner-tony@comcast.net

PROLOGUE

As it relates to this book, a "spiritually wounded warrior" is defined as (1) a *spiritual warrior* who is first and foremost a good soldier of Jesus Christ [2 Timothy 2:3]. As such, they are prepared to engage and fight against the spiritual forces of evil in the heavenly places [Ephesians 6:12]. (2) *Spiritual wounds* are invisible battle injuries that affect a warrior's heart, mind, or psyche/soul, which can be as incapacitating as physical, emotional, or moral wounds [cf. Psalm 109:22]. Thus, *spiritually wounded warriors* are Christian soldiers (whether serving in the military or not) who suffer a spiritual battle injury that can sideline them from completing their assigned mission of serving and fighting for their "Commanding officer," Jesus Christ.

The concept for this second military ministry (MILMIN) manual came from our ground-breaking work, *Spiritual Battle Rattle: God's Armor*, Military Veterans' Review of Ephesians 6:10-18. The conclusion of that volume, penned by Darren Crowden (Chief Master Sergeant, U.S. Air Force, Retired), touched on the subject—and the title of this book—*Spiritually Wounded Warriors: An Army of One Another*, as it relates to spiritual battle "injuries," "fatalities," and other adverse actions within the ranks of God's Spiritual Army, the church. Darren's distinguished military career, post-military graduate education, intensive Bible training, ministry, and mental health counseling experience, summarized the spiritual battle that every Soldier, Sailor, Airman, Marine, Coast Guardsman, and Guardian (e.g., Space Force member) is engaged wherever they are stationed, deployed, or afloat (at sea).

This book applies not only to those serving in the U.S. Armed Forces but also to all Christians worldwide. Sin's prevalence has been the scourge of humanity since the beginning of time in the Garden of Eden when the First Family, Adam and Eve, disobeyed God. Evil mars and scars our marriages, families, churches, and society. Marital unfaithfulness (i.e., adultery), divorce for any reason, sexual perversion (i.e., fornication, pornography, homosexuality, bestiality, etc.), drugs and alcohol, abortion, murder, racial intolerance … the list goes on, all of which cause physical, emotional, and spiritual wounding(s). Satan is on a relentless seek and destroy mission—an aim to maim. He plans to isolate me and you to make us easy targets. Don't let him get you alone!

The Greek word *alleon* means "one another, each other, mutually, reciprocally" [1] and occurs one hundred times in the New Testament, emphasizing the importance and necessity of personal relationships with other saved believers. However, Christians serving in the military are often assigned to remote duty locations, deployed to combat zones, or simply living in the barracks or billets with no like-minded friends or *spiritual battle buddies*. Even if one or more fellow believers are in the same or nearby units, duty obligations or combat missions take precedent over off-duty time. Thus, an isolated warrior may become lax in living for the Lord and begins to imitate their ungodly warrior mates by consuming alcohol and other drugs, using vulgar language, and other immoral, worldly behaviors. The church is vital as an army of "one another," where each member has our back and vice versa. No warfighter in their right mind would try to go it alone. Do not let the enemy isolate and pick you off—you need cover fire from your *spiritual battle buddies* (Chapter 1)—a *spiritual band of brothers and sisters* to help you fight and defeat Satan. God's spiritual warriors should never leave a fallen comrade behind.

During the battle rhythm or operational tempo of combat "against the spiritual forces of evil in the heavenly places" (Ephesians 6:12), there will be those combatants who are spiritually *wounded in action* (WIA), those *killed in action* (KIA), and warriors listed as MIA or *missing in action* (Chapter 2). Just as physical warfare often results in combat trauma and, sadly, personnel losses due to injuries or deaths, God's Army, the church, will sustain losses from spiritual trauma or death from enemy action with Satan and his Evil Forces. Sometimes these wounds are self-inflicted or can result from friendly fire (i.e., from other Christians, intentional or not, rather than directly from the enemy). Spiritual warriors can become missing in action, captured behind enemy lines (POWs), or go AWOL—Absent Without the Lord. They no longer report to spiritual formation (e.g., Bible classes or worship services).

Regrettably, the U.S. military is a proving-ground for distraught service members committing *felo-de-se* or *suicide* (from Medieval Latin, literally an "evildoer in respect to oneself"). [2] Ballooning suicide rates among military members and veterans over the past couple of decades have alarmed public health professionals. "Suicide is the second leading cause of death in the U.S. military." [3] These "invisible spiritual wounds of war" often lie dormant until something triggers flashbacks from battle experiences or traumatic brain injuries (TBI). In God's Army, *spiritual suicide* may result from untreated wounds, including unforgiven wrongs. Consequently, spiritual suffering can result in discouragement, distress, and disease because of sin.

For this book, the spiritual equivalent of PTSD may be deemed as Post Traumatic Spiritual Disorder. As already stated, Christian warfighters can suffer from the invisible wounds of spiritual combat with the evil one. They may look or act "normal" on the outside but might be carrying spiritual shrapnel in their soul. In passing, you may have heard something like this: "Hey Sarge, how are you doing today?" "Oh, I'm *okay*," or "I'm *great*, how are you?" Each person acknowledges the other but many times superficially. We wear hidden masks to cover up the hurt and struggles as we suffer silently; we are afraid to let them down or remove them for fear of embarrassment and thus keep trucking along life's highway as if nothing is wrong. In reality, they are hurt and ashamed to admit their life is second-rate and their soul is in eternal jeopardy. Spiritually speaking, they are committing *spiritual suicide* (Chapter 3).

Fires can be good or bad, depending on their usage and intent. In the military, fires mean:

> The related tasks and systems that provide collective and coordinated use of Army indirect fires, air and missile defense, and joint fires through the targeting process. Alternatively, it can be defined as the use of weapon systems to create a specific lethal or nonlethal effect on a target. [4]

In this scenario, fires are a good doctrine as they are directed toward the enemy. Regrettably, in the heat of battle, "fires or friendly fire" occur in the "fog of war." Thousands of friendly fire cases (sometimes called *fratricide*) have been reported throughout military history. Due to a decline in morale and discipline during the Vietnam War, "fragging" (use of a fragmentation grenade) was used to kill superior officers and NCOs. "Reports from Vietnam talk of demoralization and of draftees 'fragging' gung-ho officers; that is tossing hand grenades at them to put a stop to aggressiveness." [5] "Most fragging incidents were in the Army and Marine Corps. Fragging was rare among Navy and Air Force personnel, who had less access to grenades and weapons than did soldiers and marines" [6]

Friendly fire is "an attack by belligerent or neutral forces on friendly troops while attempting to attack enemy/hostile targets." [7] In other words, warfighters fire on their fellow troops instead of the enemy.

This isn't limited to the U.S. military either. For instance, a Russian soldier fighting in Ukraine kept a daily journal that detailed attacks in southern Ukraine in the hopes of telling his country the truth about the war to stop it. After being wounded and evacuated from the battlefield, he wrote on Russia's equivalent of Facebook and tells of "units being wiped out by friendly fire." [8]

There are many reasons (*excuses*, perhaps?) for these sad occurrences, whether in physical combat or spiritual warfare. In the heat of spiritual battle, when trading blows with our enemies of darkness, we might unintentionally (or deliberately) fire upon and wound our fellow soldiers of Christ. Cody Francis said,

> It is impossible to win a war if you are wounding or killing your own men and not the enemy, thus in a war, if you are going to be victorious you must know who the enemy is and who the enemy is not … Since friendly fire involves firing upon your comrade, instead of your enemy, it is imperative that we understand very clearly the true identity of the enemy. [9]

While taking one's life or suicide is the most extreme, ultimate form of self-destructive behavior, many other wanton activities or self-afflictions can wreck one's military career and life. Sporting activities like mountain or rock climbing, skydiving, or whitewater rafting fall into an elevated risk category that can impact a sailor or airman's ability to perform their job. Other precarious actions that can affect one's line of duty include using alcohol, other drugs, or aberrant sexual behaviors. Christian warriors suffer from spiritual friendly fire, and many also engage in *high-risk behaviors* that endanger and degrade their influence within their duty assignments, immediate family, and congregations. Activities like those mentioned above, such as viewing pornography, gambling, involvement in illegal activities, and others, can put one's soul in eternal jeopardy (Chapter 4).

Spiritual combat casualty care medics (Chapter 5) render aid to Christian warriors injured in the line of spiritual duty. Some may only require limited love and care of fellow saints or "battle buddies" to soothe and treat their light to moderate wounds through daily Bible reading, consistent prayer, copious encouragement, and so forth. Many qualified Christian authors have penned good books to aid in spiritual treatment. However, those suffering more severe disorders or trauma may need referral to, or consultation with, a *spiritual casualty care specialist* beyond the minister's expertise or that of the church elders or shepherds (i.e., mental health, marriage/family, alcohol, or sexual addiction counseling).

When a warfighter suffers a severe injury in the heat of battle, they or their battle-brothers typically cry out, "Medic!" I remember watching the epic WWII movie "Saving Private Ryan," starring Tom Hanks, as wave after wave of U.S. soldiers hit Omaha beach in Normandy, France, on D-Day (June 6, 1944) under the violent volley of enemy artillery and bullets whizzing all around. Countless courageous combatants fell dead as they waded into the waters and approached the shoreline, while untold others sustained traumatic battle injuries to the painful cries of "Medic!" Without these trained first aid responders who render emergent frontline care, warriors may well lose hope of getting home alive. These first-aid heroes or combat corpsmen provide initial battle care during the "golden hour" following a traumatic injury when there is the highest likelihood that prompt medical and surgical treatment will prevent death. Once a wounded warrior is medically evacuated or medevac'd off the battlefield, they are transported to the rear echelon for more definitive care by professional medical specialists.

Similarly, Christian warriors wounded in action while serving on the frontlines in God's Army need prompt emergency first aid and follow-on care in varying *spiritual echelons* (levels) *of care* (Chapter 6): individual Christians – "spiritual stretcher-bearers" for the wounded – that is, preachers, youth ministers, elders/shepherds, or trained professional counselors. Charles Hodge, a well-known gospel preacher, spoke at a military church retreat in Berchtesgaden, Germany (on the former site of Hitler's SS [Schutzstaffel or "Protection Echelon"] Headquarters during the Cold War years) that I attended in the late 1980s said, "The church is an emergency room God runs for sinners." [10]

No one is immune from sustaining injuries or death on the battlefield. Officers of all levels (general or flag officers, field grade or senior officers, company, junior grade, and warrant officers) have sustained severe and deadly battle wounds. For instance, American general and flag officers died in action in WWII in the European Theater (ETO) and the Pacific Theater (PTO) of Operations. [11] More recently, "Maj. Gen. Greene [two stars] is the highest-ranking officer to have been killed in either Iraq or Afghanistan." [12] Non-commissioned and petty officers and lower enlisted personnel have all sustained and/or died from their battle injuries. I point this out because every Christian in God's Army (including elders, deacons, preachers, ministry staff, Bible teachers, and others in the pews) is susceptible to, and can succumb, to battle injuries with the evil forces of darkness. This truth is critical to our understanding as we sometimes view our leaders as super-Christians who are seemingly indestructible because of their strong faith. When they sin and fail us, our faith in them is shaken or broken, and we wonder why. When that happens to our leaders, they also need treatment, healing, and restoration from the Great Physician.

During combat operations (and even in the "quieter" moments of warfare), ground forces are especially in danger of suffering battle wounds that can produce lasting scars which remind the injured warrior (and others) of the uncertainty and ugly side of warfare. Physical battle scars can often be minimized through multiple plastic surgeries, whereas invisible wounds like traumatic brain injuries (TBI) may never be erased; they too require additional surgeries and various cognitive therapies and medications. Emotional scars resulting from PTSD may last a lifetime and contribute to many residual problems after discharge from the service. In WWII, such emotional wounds were called "combat/battle fatigue or shell shock," which sometimes led to "lethal lassitude" (i.e., helplessness resulting in death) if left untreated. Likewise, *spiritual battle scars* (Chapter 7) from combat with Satan and his evil forces can also be long-lasting. God's wounded warriors require spiritual therapies and disciplines such as prayer, quiet personal time and meditation on His word, in-depth Bible study, Christian counseling, and close fellowship with loving, like-minded brothers and sisters to aid their healing.

When soldiers, airmen, sailors, or Marines sustain injuries on the battlefield, they are initially treated by a medical corpsman (Army) or hospital corpsman (Navy) trained in Tactical Combat Casualty Care. If their wounds or conditions are acute or emergent, they will be transferred to a higher echelon or level of care for further evaluation and treatment. If a warrior feels ill or suffers an injury, they report to "sick call" at a troop medical clinic, battalion aid station, or Navy sickbay to receive medical care. Conditions may range from a simple cold to a sprained ankle or back pain to a more severe disorder or injury requiring prompt attention in the Emergency Room. While there, a combat medic or hospital duty corpsmen may administer various over-the-counter drugs to treat minor illnesses. They may also utilize assorted splints, bandages, tourniquets, and other resources to initially treat or stabilize their patient (pre-hospital) until transferred to more definitive care.

Military physicians, physician's assistants, or nurse practitioners diagnose and prescribe medications, including controlled substances, for various illnesses or diseases for more severe conditions or injuries. These professionals may transfer traumatic injuries or acute diseases to advanced specialists for more definitive care, surgery, and further treatment plans. Treatment plans include proper nutrition (i.e., vitamin or herbal supplements), adequate sleep, and physical exercise. Likewise, God's warriors who are sick or wounded in action need appropriate *spiritual medicine and treatment plans* (Chapter 8). To restore and maintain their spiritual strength from an illness or injury, Christians need a regular, balanced diet of the Bible (both Old and New Testaments). Jesus expressed, "Blessed are those who hunger and thirst for righteousness, for they shall be satisfied" (Matthew 5:6). Like POWs deprived of physical food and water are weakened to the point of death, a wounded Christian who no longer desires spiritual food and drink will die eternally.

After an ill or injured service member is treated by an appropriate medical specialist utilizing various medications, surgery, or other treatment modalities in a hospital setting, they must heal and recuperate. Referral for professional consultation includes nutritional, occupational, physical, and/or speech therapists who design a plan of care for rehabilitation to prepare the warrior for return to duty or medical discharge/retirement if the service member can no longer perform their military duties.

Recovery and rehabilitation are integral to healing an injured warrior in physical combat (physical or emotional trauma). God's soldier who experiences spiritual injury or trauma also requires appropriate spiritual revival and rehabilitation to restore them to duty. *Spiritual recovery* (Chapter 9) is an essential component for a Christian soldier to fully regain their strength and readiness to perform their assigned mission (i.e., living and serving Christ, sharing the gospel with others, etc.), as well as the ability to bounce back after emotional injury or trauma. "The physical, mental, social, and spiritual domains of fitness build and maintain the toughness and resiliency necessary to adapt to, overcome, and recover from every situation Marines and Sailors face in their careers." [13]

During my active duty years in the 1970s and 1980s, wounded or injured soldiers were assigned to Medical Holding Units during their recovery phase or processing out of the Army by medical review boards. In the fall of 2020, the Army *Warrior Transition Units* ("Med Hold") became *Soldier Recovery Units*. This new recovery program held "reflagging ceremonies" throughout the Army to highlight this change. "Every day, they approach their recoveries with bold determination, and we are committed to doing the same as we provide them with the vital support and resources needed to truly overcome." [14] Whether treating battle-hardened warriors injured in spiritual combat or those who have yet to experience the healing power of their sins through their initial obedience to Christ, His location for those suffering from all sorts of battle wounds is the *church*—a Spiritual Treatment Facility and Spiritual Wounded Warrior Regiment.

All military personnel hope and long for peace, an end to the war so they can go home and reunite with their loved ones with whom they have been separated for long periods. I am sure you, like me, have witnessed on television or social media the joy of returning warriors as they step off the plane, ship, and bus to the cheers and waiting arms for hugs and kisses they have missed for so long.

On May 8, 1945 - known as Victory in Europe Day or V-E Day – celebrations erupted around the world to mark the end of World War II in Europe ... But in his speech to the nation on V-E Day, President Harry S. Truman cautioned that Allies must 'work to finish the war' by defeating the Japanese in the Pacific [15] ... V-J Day, or Victory over Japan Day, marks the end of World War II, one of the deadliest and most destruction [sic] wars in history. When ... Truman announced on August 14, 1945, that Japan surrendered unconditionally, war-weary citizens around the world erupted in celebration. [16]

Spiritually speaking, war-weary Christians will have cause to rejoice when this world ends with defeating humanity's greatest enemy, Satan, and his evil forces. While no one knows when this will happen, rest assured that the spiritual warfare you have struggled to remain engaged in will end in *Victory in Jesus or V-J Day* (Chapter 10).

During U.S. military operations in Iraq and Afghanistan, Military OutReach and Encouragement (M.O.R.E.) in Huntsville, Alabama, sent hundreds of care packages and literally thousands of cards, letters, and innumerable prayers to deployed warfighters, including federal employees and contractors. One contract servicer, "Chip," recently shared the following with me on Facebook:

> You sure made it a lot less lonely in Iraq and Afghanistan, those cards and letters and especially knowing that group [M.O.R.E.] was praying for me brought a little light to a really challenging time in my life. This wasn't just war for me either, it was post-divorce and a lot of hurting. Thank you if I have never told you. Also thank you for including contractors.

Hopefully, this comprehensive overview, the second book of our series on *Spiritual Warriors*, captures the essence, the essentiality, and the earnestness for military ministry in today's fast-paced, ever-changing, and challenging environment of sea deployment, garrison life, and combat environs. The men who penned these chapters are all experts in the respective military and civilian job specialties. All are faithful soldiers in God's Army who have experienced spiritual battle wounds and subsequent scars. Each author writes from their unique perspective, accrued wisdom, and personal stories woven into this spiritual battle manual.

On the eve of publishing this labor of love, I came across the following excerpt from the Stars and Stripes about "moral injury" that supports the need for military ministry and, thus, our efforts.

> Moral injury refers to the distress that people feel after committing an act that violates their sense of right and wrong or being forced to experience immoral actions by someone else … 'Veterans suffering from moral injury struggle with reconciling their values with the way things can unfold in times of war' … symptoms unique to moral injury include withdrawal from social life as well as changes in people's belief in their own goodness and their outlook on their purpose in life … 'PTSD, that kind of trauma is about a racing heart. Moral injury is about a broken heart' … [17]

Whether or not you presently serve, have served in the U.S. military, or deployed to a combat zone as a federal or contract employee, you are a spiritual warrior in God's Army as a Christian. As such, be ready for the *certainty* that you and/or your spiritual battle buddy (e.g., brother or sister in Christ) will become a *spiritually wounded warrior* as you fight the Evil Special Forces together daily. A vital component of battle readiness is preparing to take on and treat casualties with well-trained and well-supplied resources. Jesus has your six (i.e., back)—do you have someone else's? *Stay spiritually strong* in God's church—an Army of One Another!

ED LINEBAUGH, U.S. Army, Retired

Director, Military OutReach and Encouragement

S.E.A.L. (Spiritual Education And Leadership) Training

Huntsville, Alabama

EMAIL: more@minister.com

ENDNOTES:

1 *Alleon*. https://biblehub.com/greek/240.htm

2 *Felo-de-so*. https://www.merriam-webster.com/dictionary/felo-de-se

3 *Suicide*. https://deploymentpsych.org/disorders/suicide-main

4 *Fires*. https://en.wikipedia.org/wiki/Fires_(military)

5 *Fragging*. https://www.historynet.com/the-hard-truth-about-fragging/

6 *Fragging*. https://en.wikipedia.org/wiki/Fragging

7 *Friendly Fire*. https://en.wikipedia.org/wiki/Friendly_fire

8 *Journal*. https://www.stripes.com/theaters/europe/2022-08-21/russian-soldier-journal-ukraine

9 *Friendly Fire*. https://www.stepstolife.org/article/friendly-fire

10 *One Another*. http://www.biblecourses.com/English/en_lessons/EN_198904_13.pdf

11 *American General*. https://ww2gravestone.com/american-general-and-flag-officers-killed-in-world-war-ii/

12 *General and Flag Officers*. https://warontherocks.com/2014/08/general-and-flag-officers-killed-in-war/

13 *Resiliency and Spiritual Fitness*. https://www.marines.mil/News/Messages/Messages-Display/Article/2433271/resiliency-and-spiritual-fitness/

14 *Resiliency and Spiritual Fitness*. https://www.marines.mil/News/Messages/Messages-Display/Article/2433271/resiliency-and-spiritual-fitness/

15 *Victory in Europe*. https://www.defense.gov/Multimedia/Experience/VE-Day/

16 *Victory Over Japan*. https://www.defense.gov/Multimedia/Experience/VJ-Day/

17 *Moral Injury*. https://www.stripes.com/theaters/middle_east/2022-08-12/moral-injury-afghanistan

CHAPTER 1
Spiritual Battle Buddies

The subtitle of this book, "An Army of One Another," and the idea for this specific chapter stems from the United States Army's concept and use of soldier-partners, "battle buddies," and the short-lived recruiting motto, "An Army of One." The term "one another" or "each other" occurs one hundred times in the New Testament. "Approximately 59 of those occurrences are specific commands teaching us how (and how not to) relate to one another." [1]

Several expressions frequently used in the military reflect a personal and professional bond: comrade-in-arms, brother-in-arms, battle brother, wingman, and shipmate. For example, the Army assigns its soldiers a "battle buddy" to assist them in and out of combat, someone they can trust with their life. These cohorts are skilled in keeping an eye on one another, ensuring they do the right thing; they also provide camaraderie and a degree of emotional and physical support. This band of brothers and sisters is "not only intended for company, but also for reduction of suicide; since each watches their partner's actions … [and] can save fellow soldier's life by noticing negative thoughts and feelings and intervening to provide help." [2] Troops in God's Army likewise need camaraderie and encouragement of fellow spiritual warriors and accountability from a brother or sister's keeper.

The Department of Defense effort has implemented several preventative measures to reduce the military's increasing suicide rate in its ranks (particularly in the National Guard). This endeavor includes "access to mental health care during National Guard weekend drills, educational programs to teach life skills to young service members and increasing awareness of suicide risk factors." [3] Army General Michael X. Garrett, FORSCOM Commanding General, referring to suicide prevention in a letter to the Army Times, stated the following:

> I am here to tell you: you *do* have support, you *don't* stand alone. Don't hesitate to ask to seek help. Having grown up in a military family, and now as the Commander of the army's largest organization, I am saying with authority that this army is a family – we are brothers and sisters. We are here to lift each other up, to provide support, to listen, to ask the hard questions. [4]

All the armed services use some sort of battle buddy teams to provide peer support and accountability. In combat, these teams provide security and cover fire when on the move from one location to another. [5] Perhaps you are thinking right now that the term "battle buddy" sounds a little, shall I say, too close for comfort, too cozy, too personal ... maybe just a little *too* weird for your civilian taste. Perhaps you feel like you don't need anyone looking over your shoulder—that one person to whom you can confide and who will hold you accountable. After all, you have made it this far in your spiritual journey (more of an *adventure*). *Right?* All you need is God to forgive you just *one* more time for that habitual sin. "Please, Lord, I am sorry that I gave in to that temptation (whatever it is) again for the umpteenth time." How many times have you prayed those or similar words? How often have you beaten yourself up, crying to God to rescue you from the abyss you find yourself heading into repeatedly? Can you feel the spiritual darkness—the loneliness, the anger, the self-hatred, and the despair—that has enveloped you? Well, guess what? Despite Satan's repeated whispered lies and evil special forces, you are not alone: "God doesn't care, you're worthless;" "nobody cares what you do in the dark, it's nobody's business but yours."

Who ya gonna call—*Ghostbusters*? When confronted with troubling problems relating to our own doing or something entirely out of our control, who do *you* appeal to for help? I don't know about you but calling on God is always the sensible and righteous thing to do. Another substantial benefit in tempting times is connecting with another Christian, a battle brother or sister who has "been there, done that" – with whom you trust and can bear your soul. It is akin to calling in close air (prayer) support. Sometimes, all we need is a little extra help or aid, while at other times, we need all the reinforcements we can muster!

There is an amazing story in the Old Testament book of Exodus. Having left Egyptian slavery by God's mighty hand through His servant Moses (ever heard about the Red Sea being parted or divided?), the nation of Israel is marching toward the Promised Land of Canaan.

Along the way, God's people had to fight Amalek, one of Esau's grandsons, who became the leader of the Amalekites, an ancient band of marauders who were vicious enemies of early Israel. [6]

> Whenever Moses held up his hand, Israel prevailed, and whenever he lowered his hand, Amalek prevailed. But Moses' hands grew weary, so they took a stone and put it under him, and he sat on it, while Aaron and Hur held up his hands, one on one side, and the other on the other side. So his hands were steady until the going down of the sun. And Joshua overwhelmed Amalek and his people with the sword. (Exodus 17:11-13)

While combating our spiritual enemies, we will grow physically, mentally, and undoubtedly, spiritually exhausted like Moses likely felt, allowing the enemy to win not the war but a particular battle or skirmish. It is then we may receive severe spiritual battle wounds. We need battle buddies like Aaron and Hur to prop us up, to give us strength and encouragement that will enable us to be victorious. In the New Testament, the apostle Paul wrote: "Brothers, if anyone is caught in any transgression, you who are spiritual should restore him in a spirit of gentleness. Keep watch on yourself, lest you too be tempted. *Bear one another's burdens*, and so fulfill the law of Christ" (Galatians 6:1-2, emphasis mine, *el*).

How can you hold or prop up another brother or sister who is mentally, emotionally, and spiritually exhausted? *First*, simply letting them know you are there for them and are ready to help is often comforting. All people, including Christians, need reassurance that they are not alone in troublesome times. Discouragement is one of Satan's most effective tactics, and encouraging another person can help keep them from spiraling downward. *Secondly*, there are numerous ways to lift up a disabled, disheartened, or disengaged warrior. Prayers and encouraging words are always beneficial (let them know you are praying for them). Consider calling to check on them or send a card, email, or text (not the best but still suitable). Eating a meal together (church members are usually good at that), paying them a visit, or a simple hug (be careful with the opposite sex as they might misread your overture, and only if you know this person. It should always be a "holy" side hug with pure motives. Romans 16:16 notes, "Greet one another with a *holy* kiss" (emphasis mine, *el*).

Have you ever been caught "red-handed" or in the act of doing something wrong? I have at least twice that I recall. Like me, you probably did something as a kid and remember the ugly consequences. To be caught in a spiritual sense means "to take one by forestalling … (before he can flee or conceal his crime) … [to] surprise, detect." [7] Imagine the guilt, the shame, the anger, and the loneliness that sin produces. But we are not alone in such instances! The word "bear" means to "take up in order to carry or bear; to put upon oneself (something) to be carried; to bear what is burdensome." [8] If there is ever a need for a spiritual battle buddy, it is when we struggle with any kind of sin to the point where we can no longer handle it ourselves. Imagine how good it would feel to have another Christian "pull up underneath" to help carry your troubles. If you know what it is like to have someone help *you* in times of distress, *you* are in a perfect position to help a brother or sister in Christ. The phrase "walk a mile in his moccasins" is often credited to various Indian tribes; however, it was taken from a poem by Mary T. Lathrap in 1895. One verse conveys,

> Don't be too harsh with the man that sins.
> Or pelt him with words, or stone, or disdain.
> Unless you are sure you have no sins of your own,
> And it's only wisdom and love that your heart contains. [9]

Is it hard to share that *one* specific problem or dark secret, that deep hurt, with another Christian? Well, yes and no. From my own previous spiritual battle injury (self-inflicted) experiences, it depends on where you are on the spiritual spectrum. While stationed overseas in my early military career, our small congregation comprised of mainly young to a few older (in the faith) Christians. While it was hard to share very personal struggles at the time, we still depended on one another to get us through the daily spiritual skirmishes.

My last OCONUS duty tour was from 1986 to 1990 in Bremerhaven, a seaport city on the northern coast of Germany. No matter what happened during the week, my young family (our daughter was eight years old then) met with fellow Christians every Wednesday night for nearly four years in our apartment for Bible study. We also drove about 50 miles round trip on Friday nights for additional devotional time, games, and food with other military Christians from the 2nd Armored Division Forward in Garlstedt. That spiritual high was capped off every Sunday by worshiping God together and eating lunch afterward (except for those military brethren who were "in the field" (e.g., field training exercise) or on TDY. While we grew spiritually and enjoyed this extraordinary period of our lives, we experienced a very shallow point in our first year.

This was my second duty assignment at the 2nd Field Hospital (U.S. Army MEDDAC; the first time from 1976 to 1979). We lived two blocks from the hospital in military housing, so we were very excited to return and live across the street from our first home nearly seven years earlier. I worked in the same hospital department (orthopedics) as I did eight years prior and was thus well familiar with our surroundings. Not only this, but we also worshipped on Sundays in the same small military chapel down the block. We were "living the dream" of military ministry and excited and eager to serve the Lord with our fellow military and U.S. civilian brothers and sisters! It wasn't long, though, before I was "put in my place" by certain members of the congregation who did not take kindly to my enthusiasm. They made it very clear that *they* had been there long before we arrived and that *we* were the "new kids on the block." We were invited to lunch on our first Sunday at one of the member family's homes and then again for an Independence Day fellowship meal about two weeks later. After that, we were on our own—spiritually snubbed by those supposed saints. "Don't rock the boat," one civilian brother said. We tried many times to have others into our small apartment, but most were not interested. Why? What had we done something to offend them? We honestly didn't know. And it hurt *deep* down to our spiritual core by "friendly (or not-so-friendly) fire." My wife was most discouraged in our beloved military community that first year. We felt like we were walking through the valley of the shadow of death, spiritually speaking.

As we neared the end of that first year, I decided to do what we had never done in our two previous overseas tours—I took Kathy and our young daughter, Nicole, back to the States for a month-long R and R. We traveled back to Augusta, Georgia, and nearby Fort Gordon to spend time with very dear friends, Tommy and Pat, who were our very close spiritual family. They and the church there loved Kathy and Nicole tenderly and helped nurture them back to spiritual health. Upon our return to Bremerhaven a month later, many families had rotated back to the States at the end of their tours of duty; this included most of those who had spiritually wounded us (whether they realized it or not). The remaining three years (I extended my overseas tour by an additional year) were a pleasant and peaceful experience.

But God—have you ever noticed these two words in the Bible? Check them out. God had a wonderful surprise blessing awaiting us— He sent another military church family our way, not just *any* family. This sweet Air Force couple and their daughter were transferred from the recently-shuttered Woensdrecht Air Base (a former cruise missile facility) in Holland near the Belgian border to our Army community in

Norddeutschland (e.g., North Germany). Their names are Darren, Jennifer, and Emily (who was a year older than our daughter). Yes, Darren is a contributing author of this book and *Spiritual Battle Rattle: God's Armor*. His divine providence allowed our paths to cross to fulfill His plan through our families working together *then* and *now*. They quickly became our close spiritual battle buddies, and along with other dear saints, we bonded to form an *Army of One Another*. We lived across the hall from Darren and Jennifer in Army housing, spending countless exuberant evenings and weekends with them and other church families, eating, playing games, laughing, and crying together.

When it came time to PCS from Germany and our beloved church family, it was one of the most challenging things we have ever done. One of our favorite songs was "God's Family," which we sang innumerable times there. We tried to sing it on our last Wednesday night before driving to Rhein-Main Air Base in Frankfurt, then off to the land of round doorknobs—'Merica. There was not a dry eye that night. When we finally arrived at my new duty station in Aurora, Colorado (the former Fitzsimons Army Medical Center) in June 1990 and connected with a new church family, I wept for years trying to sing the chorus of "God's Family," "*We're part of the family ....*"

Finally, whether serving in the military or not, every Christian needs to be a spiritual battle-brother or battle-sister to fellow warriors who share a common bond—an amazing alliance. Whether you have sustained a spiritual abrasion, a moderate wound, a severe battle injury, or have non-healing scars, the church is the Ultimate Spiritual Aid Station to receive proper, soothing care. The kingdom of God, His church on earth, is not only God's spiritual emergency room; it is a respite and recovery room from the scourge of spiritual struggles secondary to sin. I hope you are blessed to have someone like Darren and Jennifer in your life. Be a *Spiritual Battle Buddy* to another Christian to help prevent spiritual combat trauma and assist other *Spiritually Wounded Warriors* as *An Army of One Another*.

ED LINEBAUGH, U.S. Army Retired
MOS: Combat Medical Specialist / Senior Orthopedic NCO
EMAIL: more@minister.com

ENDNOTES:

1 *One Another Passages*. https://www.mmlearn.org/hubfs/docs/OneAnotherPassages.pdf
2 *Battle Buddy*. https://www.definitions.net/definition/battle%20buddy
3 *Suicide Report*. https://www.cpr.org/ 2019/09/26/ department-of-defense-releases-suicide-report-as-the-military-looks-to-reduce-suicides-in-its-ranks/
4 *You don't stand alone*. https://www.army.mil/article/238804/you_dont_stand_alone_suicide_prevention_takes_teamwork_intervention
5 *Battle Buddies*. https://www.goodfellow.af.mil/Newsroom/Commentaries/Display/Article/375380/battle-buddies/
6 *Amalek*. https://www.biblegateway.com/resources/encyclopedia-of-the-bible/Amalek

7 *Bastazó*. https://biblehub.com/greek/941.htm
8 *Prolambanó*. https://biblehub.com/greek/4301.htm
9 *Walk a Mile*. https://native-americans.com/walk-mile-in-his-moccasins/

CHAPTER 2

Spiritual Battle Wounds: WIA, KIAs, and MIAs

"The spirit of a man will sustain his infirmity; but a *wounded spirit* who can bear?" (Proverbs 18:14, KJV, emphasis mine, *dc*)

During the battle rhythm or operational tempo of combat "against the rulers, against the authorities, against the cosmic powers over this present darkness, against the spiritual forces of evil in the heavenly places" (Ephesians 6:12), there will inevitably be spiritual battle injuries, mortalities, and those missing in action. Just as physical warfare often results in combat trauma and, sadly, personnel losses due to injuries or deaths, God's Army will sustain losses from spiritual trauma or death from enemy action with Satan and his evil forces. Sometimes these wounds are self-inflicted or can even result from friendly fire (i.e., from other Christians, intentional or unintentional) rather than directly from the enemy.

Wounded in action (WIA) are those combatants injured while fighting in a combat zone during wartime. It implies they are temporarily or permanently incapable of bearing arms or continuing the fight. Generally, WIAs are far more numerous than those killed.

Common combat injuries include second and third-degree burns, broken bones, shrapnel wounds, brain injuries, spinal cord injuries, nerve damage, paralysis, sight and hearing loss, post-traumatic stress disorder (PTSD), and limb loss. [1] Killed in action (KIA) is a casualty classification generally used by militaries to describe the deaths of their combatants at the hands of hostile forces. For example, the United States Department of Defense says that those declared KIA did not need to have fired their weapons but were only killed due to hostile attacks. [2]

The military also experiences loss from those listed as MIAs, which is considered an "occupational risk" or hazard.

Missing in action is a casualty classification assigned to combatants, military chaplains, combat medics, and prisoners of war who are reported missing during wartime or ceasefire. They may have been killed, wounded, captured, executed, or deserted. If deceased, neither their remains nor grave has been positively identified. [3]

The Defense Department's POW/MIA Accounting Agency's mission is to "provide the fullest possible accounting for our missing personnel from past conflicts to their families and the nation" [4]

We often become *missing in action* when we are enticed and drawn away. Unlike a single event or rapid change in the tempo of the battlefield causing capture, in our spiritual life, this usually happens over time when we choose not to pay attention to our beliefs, attitudes, and actions. The culture, through the three avenues of 1 John 2, discussed above, subtly works their way into our lives, much like Satan did with Adam and Eve. He started with just a simple question. There is a story about a youth minister walking over and sitting beside a young man at a youth retreat. They had just had some worship time around a campfire, and most had left for the evening, but this young man was still sitting alone staring into the fire. He had not been active in the youth group for some time, drifted away, and got caught up in other interests outside the church. He saw the youth minister coming over and expected a conversation about what was going on in his life. However, when the minister sat down, he didn't say a word for some time. Then, he grabbed a stick and pulled out a good-sized red-hot ember from the middle of the fire to just beyond it. They sat there and watched it slowly fade away to black.

An interesting statistic comes from Lifeway Research, based in Nashville, Tennessee. They surveyed why 18- to 22-year-olds dropped out of the church. While various reasons were given, the one statement that caught my attention was, "But leaving was not an intentional decision for many. Of those who dropped out, 71 percent said they did not plan on it." [5] In other words, it just happened. Maybe so. Often heard in the military is: "a failure to plan is a plan to fail." Intentionality is key. "I will study your commandments and reflect on your ways. I will delight in your decrees and not forget your word" (Psalm 119:15-16, NLT). Church can become ritualistic and seemly dogmatic if we are not careful. The "delight" mentioned in Psalm 119 is the goal. If you do a word search on "delight," you might be inspired to dig in a little harder:

- "I delight to do Your will" (Psalm 40:8).

- "His delight is in the law of the Lord, and in His law he meditates day and night" (Psalm 1:1-2).

- "Has the Lord as great delight in burnt offerings and sacrifices, as in obeying the voice of the Lord? Behold, to obey is better than sacrifice, and to heed than the fat of rams" (1 Samuel 15:22).

- "The sacrifice of the wicked is an abomination to the Lord, but the prayer of the upright is His delight" (Proverbs 15:8, NASB).

Are you spiritually MIA? What does that feel like to you right now? Remember the dead ember at the foot of the young man? After the last bit of glow had faded from the ember, the youth minister reached over with his foot, kicked the ember back to the center of the fire, and then got up and left the young man to his thoughts. Within seconds the ember flared up red hot as before, surrounded by a sea of glowing embers.

Crazy way to start the chapter given these definitions, I know. Have you ever watched the flag-draped coffins of our military members who gave the ultimate sacrifice, being off-loaded from a C-130 or some other aircraft? Just typing it gives me a sad feeling inside. Have you ever been around a wounded warrior from any of our hostilities? Maybe they are missing an eye, hand, arm, or even a leg. Or two. Perhaps they struggle on the inside with PTSD or depression, or high anxiety. Have you ever felt awkward at that moment? What do you say as an opener? Do they want to talk about it or not? You don't know where they might be in their struggle, and you might call attention to something they are not ready to address. Or maybe they are just waiting for someone to say anything to start the conversation.

We have come a long way from the days of our returning veterans from Vietnam, who were greeted with anger and hostility and called warmongers and baby killers. Vietnam vets hid in the shadows for decades and did nothing to call attention to their military service. One such veteran is Steve Duske.

> For decades, he tried to hide the fact that he was a Vietnam vet, only starting to wear his Cavalry hat about 4 years ago. Duske, who served two terms in the Army in Vietnam, said it was especially difficult watching the 1991 ticker tape parade in New York for returning Gulf War veterans. For him, that moment brought painful memories of his own return to the U.S. back to the surface. 'When they had the ticker tape parade in New York, I sat on the corner of my bed and cried,' Duske said. 'I looked at the heroes who came back from that short war, and they were given a parade. I snuck home. There was nobody at the airport. I took a taxi home.'
> 6

It sort of gives new meaning to the phrase "walking wounded." Veterans from all wars are now welcomed home, honored, and praised for their service to our country and enjoy the well-earned thankfulness from a grateful nation. It has been a much-needed change. Our spiritual wounds are not very different from our WIA counterparts. You cannot see those wounds for the most part. They manifest themselves in our spirits, take residence in our hearts and occupy our minds to utter ruin. Oh, we hide them well because, like the Vietnam veteran returning home, we are not sure how our brothers and sisters will act toward us when we crack the door open on our struggle. We hear from the pulpit the call to "come as you are" and that there are those waiting to pray with you, study with you, and walk with you in your struggle, but you are just unsure of its truth. Physical injuries do not get better by themselves, right? Neither do spiritual ones. Both have this in common—they will eventually cause death if left untreated (KIA).

Spiritual battle wounds happen due to sin, either ours or the sins of others. And that is no small thing indeed. Every day we live on planet earth is a day lived on the spiritual battlefield. John 10:10 says in part, "The thief comes only to steal and kill and destroy." If you have chosen to follow Jesus, spiritual wounding is almost inevitable. Nevertheless, we are not left to fend for ourselves. (This would be a great place to stop and read the first book in our military ministry series, *Spiritual*

Battle Rattle: God's Armor, Military Veterans' Review of Ephesians 6:10-18, if you have not done so.)

Jesus Christ came before us, leaving us light for our path, His Word of truth. In its pages, we will see the source of our spiritual wounds, how to bind and heal them and be even stronger for the fight ahead. Jesus said in John 16:33: "I have said these things to you, that in me you may have peace. In the world you will have tribulation. But take heart; I have overcome the world." What more appropriate place to start looking for the cause of spiritual wounds than "in this world."

THE SOURCE

Spiritual wounds can happen quickly (like being shot) or over time (like slow-acting poison or infection). Search for "Slow Fade" by a Christian music group called Casting Crowns and give it a listen. It basically says that nothing good fades quickly but happens bit by bit. We realize one day that we are nursing a spiritual wound more often than not. Some of these injuries result from spoken words. They might be called verbal or emotional abuse—words spoken out of fear, blame, or hate—or unspoken when they were most desperately needed, comfort, encouragement, or love. Since hurtful words (or the absence of positive comments) cause emotional or spiritual injury, words can also cure them, but to do so, they must be the right words at the right time. Another level of spiritual wounds includes physical, emotional, and sexual abuse. Healing of the physical aspect of these wounds can happen relatively quickly, but usually, the attached emotional or psychological wounds take longer to heal, if ever they do. Since actions were the cause of the injuries, actions can also cure them, but to do so, they must be the right actions at the right time.

The more fundamental source of our wounding, whether by others or self-inflicted, is described in 1 John 2:15-17. "For all that is in the world—the desires of the flesh and the desires of the eyes and pride of life—is not from the Father but is from the world." When tempted in these three ways, we open ourselves to wounding; indeed, when others in our lives are similarly tempted, we can be swept up in their consequences and wounded in the process. These have been around since the days of creation. Satan used them in the garden to hurt the first (physical) Adam and then again on the second (spiritual) Adam, e.g., Jesus (1 Corinthians 15:45-49) but not with the same outcome. And we should learn something from that.

Satan initially approached Eve through the lust of the flesh when he said, "Did God actually say, 'You shall not eat of any tree in the garden'? And the woman said to the serpent, 'We may eat of the fruit of the trees in the garden, but God said, 'You shall not eat of the fruit of the tree that is in the midst of the garden, neither shall you touch it, lest you die'" (Genesis 3:1-3). But Satan had already planted the doubt and piqued her appetite for the forbidden fruit. "So when the woman saw that the tree was good for food, and that it was a delight to the eyes," she yielded to the lust of her flesh and passed it along to her husband so that they both sinned (Genesis 3:6-7).

Satan tried the same with Jesus, tempting Him to turn stones into bread after fasting for forty days. Satan is not omniscient or all-knowing, but he is not blind either. He "prowls around as a roaring lion" (1 Peter 5:8). Where do you think the Devil prowls or stalks around? Here in this physical realm, of course. We know from the first chapter of Job that Satan can traverse the different realms or jurisdictions of earth. He is an invisible observer of all that goes on here, including you and me. And he knows that temptation is most significant when we are hungry, fatigued, and when loneliness is extreme in our lives.

The lust of the flesh—that is, *temptation*—draws us away from the will of God to serve our physical desires (see Galatians 5:16-21 and James 1:13-16). While there was nothing sinful about Eve eating *per se*, and nothing intrinsically evil about the God-forbidden fruit, it was off the table (pun intended). However, Jehovah had clearly said, "do not eat it," but Eve and her husband, Adam, chose to violate His will, acting independently of Him by consuming it. Similarly, there was nothing wrong with Jesus ending His fast with a loaf of bread, but He was not about to act independently of the Father's will by accepting Satan's offer.

The devil uses the *lust of the eyes* as well. This temptation mode subtly draws us away from God's Word and erodes our confidence in Him. We see what the world offers and desire it above our relationship with God. We place more credence or faith in our perspective of life than in His commands and promises. Fueled by lust or intense desire for what we see, we go for all we can acquire, believing that we need it and deceived that God wants us to have it. He said that death would accompany disobedience, but Satan said, "You will not surely die" (Genesis 3:4). He essentially told Eve, "Do not listen to Him; trust what you see in front of you, surely He did not mean you would actually die." Verse six tells us the forbidden fruit was a *visual delight*, so she and Adam ignored God's command to do what appeared to serve and satisfy their interest. When Satan asked Jesus to prove He was the Son of God by throwing Himself down to see if the angels would respond to His distress, he was essentially telling Jesus the same thing: trust what you see in front of you; is God *really* going to intervene to keep you from stumbling? Will He really keep His promises, both good ones and those of any negative consequence?

And lastly, the *pride of life* reared its head in the garden of Eden. "For God knows that when you eat of it your eyes will be opened, and you will be like God, knowing good and evil" (Genesis 3:5). In other words, do not be satisfied ruling under God when you have the potential to be *like* God. Back to verse 6: "the tree was to be desired to make one wise." Satan used the same temptation with Jesus when offering Him all the kingdoms of the world and resultant glory if He would only worship him (that is, Satan). The lie was that Jesus could be His own ruler. Satan tries to entice and lure you away from worshiping God and urges you to take charge of your own life, leading you down the path that you do not need God's help or direction.

Spiritual wounds or injuries will come when you or others in your orbit of relationships give in to these three areas, negating God's will, leading you away from obeying His Word, and from worship due only to God.

HOW TO BIND (BANDAGE) AND HEAL

To begin the healing process, you first need to know the source of your injury. Has it come from you or others? Once you determine that, the road to healing is slightly more transparent. For the sake of space, I will address only self-inflicted wounds, as this is where most of our injuries derive. For our personal sins, the most individualized verse in the Bible, crafted just for you and you alone, is 1 Corinthians 10:13, "No temptation has overtaken YOU that is not common to man. God is faithful, and he will not let YOU be tempted beyond YOUR ability, but with the temptation he will also provide the way of escape, that YOU may be able to endure it" (emphasis mine, *dc*). Four woundings in one verse—must be some kind of record and, more importantly, a divine message for you and me.

God the Father knows Your struggles; He knows Your weaknesses, what brings You joy and sorrow, Your emotional state and what sets it off, Your innermost thoughts, and Your breaking point—in short, He knows YOU. What an incredible promise from THE Promise Keeper. No one else seems to struggle like You do. Yes, as the verse states, we have mutual struggles familiar to us all, but how YOU respond to it may affect YOU is unique in many ways. Spiritual wounds are like that. Two people may experience the same type of injury but react very differently. Your personality, perception of your surroundings, and how you process or think about things make you like no other. However, look at the verse closely. It does not say that God gives us a way out from temptation so that it stops; instead, He provides us with the means of escape to bear or shoulder our particular temptation and NOT sin or be wounded by such.

James 1:14 and 15 help illustrate this. Verse 14 states, "But each person is tempted when he is lured and enticed by his own desire." Verse 15 says, "Then desire when it has conceived gives birth to sin, and sin when it is fully grown brings forth death." There is an action here – *conceive*. Desire has the ability to create or give birth to sin. How? When you give into and act upon that particular desire. Picture, if you will, 1 Corinthians 10:13 in between James 1:13 and 15. This can help you endure or stand under the temptation and not give into it. Consider these interrelated Bible verses:

- "But each person is tempted when he is lured and enticed by his own desire" (James 1:14).

- "No temptation has overtaken you that is not common to man. God is faithful, and he will not let you be tempted beyond your ability, but with the temptation he will also provide the way of escape, that you may be able to endure it" (1 Corinthians 10:13).

- "Then desire when it has conceived gives birth to sin, and sin when it is fully grown brings forth death" (James 1:15).

But again, how does that work? Back to the book of James, this time, chapter 4 and verse 7: "Submit yourselves therefore to God. Resist the devil, and he will flee from you." Note two required actions of us: (1) *submit* to God and (2) *resist* the devil. The result: he (Satan) will flee. Where else are we told what to do to cause this fallen angel, this powerful spiritual being, this roaring lion, this being who has been in the presence of God and who has caused untold chaos to the human race over the centuries—to escape or run away? I believe that when we "submit" to God, we "resist" Satan, which is the same action. Something to think about, eh?

HOW TO BE STRONG FOR THE FIGHT AHEAD

Strength comes through discipline, subjecting our bodies and minds to some pain. You have heard the phrase "no pain, no gain." No difference here. God's discipline is an oft-ignored fact of life for believers. We often complain about our circumstances without realizing that they are the consequences of our sin and part of the Lord's discipline. This ignorance can contribute to the formation of habitual sin, bringing even greater discipline and pain.

The Lord's discipline comes from His love and desire for us to be holy like Him. "My son, do not despise the LORD's discipline and do not resent his rebuke, because the LORD *disciplines those he loves*, as a father the son he delights in" (Proverbs 3:11-12, NIV, emphasis mine, *dc*). God will use testing, trials, and various predicaments to bring us back to Himself in repentance. His discipline results in a stronger faith and a renewed relationship with Him (cf. James 1:2-4). The Lord corrects us for our good so that He might be glorified with how we live. He wants us to exhibit holiness, lives that reflect the new nature or character He gives us: "As obedient children, do not be conformed to the passions of your former ignorance, but as he who called you is holy, you also be holy in all your conduct, since it is written, 'You shall be holy, for I am holy'" (1 Peter 1:14-16).

There is an object lesson for all of us. Consider the Japanese art of Kintsugi. This word means "golden joinery," a method of repairing broken ceramics with a lacquer mixed with gold, silver, or platinum. The aim is not to hide the repairs but to make them a feature—to incorporate them into a more beautiful design than the original. Its philosophy is to value the brokenness and restoration as part of the object's history rather than seeing it as something to disguise. In contrast to Western philosophy, which strives for perfection and looks to hide brokenness, Kintsugi acknowledges the brokenness and pieces it back together into something beautiful. A delightful work of art that is worth much more than the original.

In conclusion, if you are spiritually wounded, whether by your own doing, from friendly fire (i.e., those in the body of Christ, modeling Christ imperfectly), or by others, know that you are not alone. God can heal YOUR wounds; all the cracks and imperfections will become part of who YOU are, molded under Him into a beautiful design. He is the original Kintsugi Artist! Psalms 147:3 says, "He heals the brokenhearted and binds up their wounds." May you allow Him to do so with you—now and always.

DARREN CROWDEN, U.S. Air Force, Retired

AFSC: Administrative Superintendent

EMAIL: cnerrad@yahoo.com

EDITOR'S NOTE: Darren has a Master of Arts in Mental Health Counseling, specializing in Sexual Addictions. He uses his education and ample experience to minister within and outside the church.

ENDNOTES:

1 *Costs of War*. https://watson.brown.edu/costsofwar/costs/human/military/wounded

2 *Killed in Action*. https://en.wikipedia.org/wiki/Killed_in_action

3 *Missing in Action*. https://www.dpaa.mil/Our-Missing/Past-Conflicts/

4 *Missing in Action*. https://en.wikipedia.org/wiki/Missing_in_action

5 *Dropout*. https://research.lifeway.com/2022/06/13/who-is-the-new-church-dropout/

6 *Attitudes*. http://www.vietamericanvets.com/Page-Records-Attitude-Towards-Veterans.htm.

CHAPTER 3
Spiritual Suicide

Someone said, "suicide is a permanent solution to a temporary problem." I am not sure to whom I should credit that statement, but it is accurate and tragic. Unfortunately, when a person takes their own life, they cannot reverse the consequences. I often wonder if people regret their attempt to kill themselves at some point. Those who use a gun often tend not to fail in their attempt because these weapons tend to do the job more quickly and adequately. However, for those who end up dying a slower death, I wonder if they have any regrets once they can feel their demise is approaching.

Working as an Army Religious Affairs Specialist, I have known many soldiers who have contemplated and attempted suicide; unfortunately, many have succeeded in their efforts. In my career, I have attended over sixty memorials for soldiers who committed suicide; almost all were in a non-combat environment. I bring that up because we can apply that to our thoughts on *spiritual suicide*.

I believe most attempted suicides are outside the combat environment because service members can contemplate their lives and worry about things outside war and fighting. In a combat situation, you have a clear purpose and a direction. Most soldiers who do not perform their actual jobs while in garrison (i.e., not deployed in combat) sometimes have too much extra time on their hands, feeling like they have no purpose. Conversely, they perform their jobs to succeed in battles or skirmishes while deployed in combat. Even those not in a role directly tied to a war zone still feel like they are contributing to the fight as they may be feeding the troops, providing logistical support, or maybe just caring for those wounded in action (WIA). Regardless, every soldier feels involved and more important while in a battle environment.

Physical combat correlates very well with a spiritual point of view. Paul says in 2 Timothy 2:3-4, "Share in suffering as a good soldier of Christ Jesus. No soldier gets entangled in civilian pursuits, since his aim is to please the one who enlisted him." Although not many scriptures distinguish soldiers from civilian life, the comparison and contrast here are very profound. A soldier never feels more influential and important than when he assists his comrades in fighting to win the war! This feeling of being valued is magnified in spiritual warfare. Those who commit or contemplate spiritual suicide involve themselves too heavily in "civilian" or worldly affairs.

What exactly is "civilian affairs?" In the military, it is drilled into us that we are soldiers 24-7-365, which means that even when we are not in uniform, we represent the United States Army wherever we go, or at least we should be. From a spiritual standpoint, "civilian affairs" means being caught up in the world (we might call them "Satan's affairs"), which means that you are not just living among the general populace or the world but living like or imitating them! Thus, Paul says that as "good soldiers of Christ Jesus," we are not to get "entangled in civilian or worldly affairs."

The apostle Peter mentions a similar type of dilemma: "For if, after they have escaped the defilements of the world through the knowledge of our Lord and Savior Jesus Christ, they are again entangled in them and overcome, the last state has become worse for them than the first" (2 Peter 2:20). If we do not act as good warriors of Christ and become intertwined with sinful activities, we are committing slow spiritual suicide! Spiritual warriors who become caught in these things are more susceptible because they are no longer in the fight!

Being in the Army means we do not choose when or where we are assigned or deployed to a combat zone. However, as a soldier of Christ, we LIVE in a spiritual combat zone daily! There is no garrison or non-combat environment. If we live like civilians (i.e., sinners in our comparison), we have broken our enlistment contract in the Lord's Army and joined the enemy. In verse 21, Peter adds, "For it would have been better for them never to have known the way of righteousness than after knowing it to turn back from the holy commandment delivered to them." A similar warning is in Hebrews 6:4-6,

It is impossible for those who have once been enlightened, who have tasted the heavenly gift, who have shared in the Holy Spirit, who have tasted the goodness of the word of God and the powers of the coming age and who have fallen away, to be brought back to repentance. To their loss they are crucifying the Son of God all over again and subjecting him to public disgrace. (NIV)

The Hebrews writer refers to what we have labeled "spiritual suicide." The more a soldier of Christ gets involved in "civilian (Satan's) affairs," the more likely they will leave their post and go AWOL. This means a Christian has rejected God's Army or church, leaves without official authorization, and does not tell anyone where they are. The longer soldiers stay away, they will officially be considered deserters (cf. MIA). "Service members accused of desertion may undergo such allegations as a result of a variety of action, which constitutes the active and purposeful disavowal from service in the United States Armed Forces." [1] The Hebrew text says that it is "impossible" for those who have fallen away to be brought back to repentance. I do not want to contradict that, but I will add the following.

When a Christian has gone spiritually AWOL (Absent Without the Lord) or is now involved in "Satan's affairs," this does not necessarily mean they have committed spiritual suicide. We, as fellow soldiers, do not and cannot determine that, but God alone will. Our job is to try and bring that person back to our CO or Commanding Officer (e.g.,

Jesus Christ) and urge them to continue serving as a soldier of Christ (this may be where the comparison falls apart a little). In the U.S. Army, an AWOL soldier will be punished with a demotion or maybe even prosecution under the UCMJ. God will not condemn you for straying and returning to Him (i.e., repenting), but there may still be consequences. However, the basic premise is that a soldier would try to help and bring that fellow soldier back, not prosecuting so much as to repair and restore!

I like Paul's comparison of the "soldier of Christ." There is so much there that can show us how to avoid spiritual suicide if we will strive to "please our commanding officer" (Jesus), as Paul states, and simply live and fight the battle for His cause. Most of the time, when one contemplates spiritual suicide, they have removed themselves from the fight and gotten too involved in civilian affairs. Satan can trick us into thinking that civilian life is an easier or better road to follow. That is why many in the military go AWOL or even just get out (sometimes early) because they no longer want to be accountable to anyone else, having to show up and follow all the rules and regulations the Army imposes. However, God's spiritual Army (church) is not this way. It is not only about following directions but having a personal, intimate relationship with our Commanding Officer (e.g., Jesus Christ) and fellowship with other spiritual warriors.

When Army units have a stern yet compassionate, fair, and approachable commander, soldiers will often bend over backward for them. When soldiers see they are cared for, they will not want to leave. In God's Army, we have a much more significant and better Leader than we find in the U.S. Armed Forces! Why would any soldier of Christ want to disobey or disrespect their CO, leave their spiritual unit (church), and jeopardize their eternal soul and wellbeing?

How do we keep ourselves from falling prey to civilian affairs? We must understand that Satan never quits; he will never give up trying to convince us that being outside God's Army is much better. Therefore, another soldier-comparison is found in Ephesians 6:10-20, where the apostle Paul lays out God's spiritual battle rattle or full armor. We all have most likely read or heard about it, at the very least. Though he does not use the phrase "soldier of Christ," we get a glimpse of how a warrior ready for battle looks! Reread this passage and keep in mind all that we have discussed so far and how it shows us how to keep us from getting involved in civilian or Satan's affairs. Read in the mindset of Paul's words, "good soldier of Christ," in the following passage (I know this is a long section of verses, but please read them in their entirety for a clear understanding of this chapter, *Spiritual Suicide* and how it relates to the overall book, *Spiritually Wounded Warriors: An Army of One Another*).

[10] Finally, be strong in the Lord and in his mighty power. [11] Put on the full armor of God, so that you can take your stand against the

devil's schemes. ¹²For our struggle is not against flesh and blood, but against the rulers, against the authorities, against the powers of this dark world and against the spiritual forces of evil in the heavenly realms. ¹³Therefore put on the full armor of God, so that when the day of evil comes, you may be able to stand your ground, and after you have done everything, to stand. ¹⁴Stand firm then, with the belt of truth buckled around your waist, with the breastplate of righteousness in place, ¹⁵and with your feet fitted with the readiness that comes from the gospel of peace. ¹⁶In addition to all this, take up the shield of faith, with which you can extinguish all the flaming arrows of the evil one. ¹⁷Take the helmet of salvation and the sword of the Spirit, which is the word of God.¹⁸And pray in the Spirit on all occasions with all kinds of prayers and requests. With this in mind, be alert and always keep on praying for all the Lord's people. (Ephesians 6:10-18, NIV)

Can you connect what Paul says in Second Timothy chapter two about a "good soldier of Christ" to what you just read above? We must be ready for battle! To win the fight against the evil surrounding us, we must put on all the *right* armor, the *full* armor, the *correct* weapons, and the *entire* equipment – God's complete body armor (read *Spiritual Battle Rattle: God's Armor*, that is available on Amazon). When I deployed to Iraq and Afghanistan, we never left our staging area without our complete battle rattle! How much more important is it for the spiritual warrior? We often commit spiritual suicide because we have not prepared, dressed as soldiers, and maintained battle-readiness! We have not trained as a soldier who is *in* the fight! We often act like we are not in a spiritual battle for the eternal souls of men and women; instead, we are like unprepared civilians! We have allowed Satan's affairs to deceive us, and we go spiritual AWOL!

What else can we do as good soldiers of Christ without getting deceived by Satan's affairs? We learn that we have "battle buddies" from Army basic training. In a nutshell, this means that we have someone battling alongside us. We have a fellow soldier who will help pick us up when we are down and bandage our wounds to help us stay in the fight. We should be there for each other, forgive each other, and be united for the cause of Christ. As U.S. soldiers in a combat zone, we must be on the same page, teamed to win America's wars. It is even more critical that we are partners in God's Army as soldiers for Christ!

Listen and read the following verses from Ephesians and Colossians and view them as a "good soldier of Christ." "I therefore, a prisoner for the Lord, urge you to walk in a manner worthy of the calling to which you have been called, with all humility and gentleness, with patience, bearing with one another in love, eager to maintain the unity of the Spirit in the bond of peace" (Ephesians 4:1-3). Colossians 3:12-15 says,

> Put on then, as God's chosen ones, holy and beloved, compassionate hearts, kindness, humility, meekness, and patience, bearing with one another and, if one has a complaint against another, forgiving each other; as the Lord has forgiven you, so you also must forgive. And above all these put on love,

which binds everything together in perfect harmony. And let the peace of Christ rule in your hearts, to which indeed you were called in one body. And be thankful.

Unity and love within God's Army are how we keep each other from committing spiritual suicide! We have a loving and compassionate "Commanding Officer" and "spiritual battle buddies," other Christian soldiers we can rely on and vice versa. We must remind each other that we are in a raging battle of our souls, that we must check our battle rattle, and make sure we are ready for the next skirmish! It is unlike any war the world has ever seen! It is unlike any physical conflict because we fight to win a conventional war. But in this spiritual war, our Commanding Officer has already won.

In conclusion, daily battles in our spiritual lives will continue; Satan will try and deceive us that he hasn't lost the war! Getting involved in civilian affairs will get us caught by the enemy. It will cause us to forget to put on a piece of armor we may need that day. We fight the daily battles to keep us safe from Satan's deception. We must battle and fight, knowing the war has already been won! We must support each other as *spiritual battle buddies* so we can all celebrate the heavenly victory awaiting us when our Commanding Officer returns to lead us home!

ALBERT FLORES, United States Army, Active Duty

MOS: Religious Affairs Specialist (aka Chaplain's Assistant)

EMAIL: alpat78@gmail.com

EDITOR'S NOTE: Albert is the U.S. soldier featured on the cover of "*Spiritual Battle Rattle: God's Armor,*" Military Veterans' Review of Ephesians 6:10-18, and a contributing author of that volume.

ENDNOTE:

1 *Desertion.* https://military.laws.com/desertion

CHAPTER 4

Spiritually Friendly Fire and High-Risk Behaviors

All Scripture references are from the New Living Translation unless indicated otherwise.

EDITOR'S ANNOTATION: Definitions for this chapter are, (a) *friendly fire*: the firing of weapons from one's forces or those of an ally primarily when resulting in the accidental death or injury of one's personnel." [1] (b) *high-risk behaviors*: "acts that increase the risk of disease or injury, which can subsequently lead to disability, death, or social problems." [2] Thus, *spiritually friendly fire* and *high-risk behaviors* are those incidents and actions from fellow Christians or themselves (sometimes events) that place one in spiritual jeopardy and retard one's lasting influence and spiritual growth.

1 *Friendly Fire*. https://www.merriam-webster.com/dictionary/ friendly%20fire

2 *High Risk Behavior*. https://www.ncbi.nlm.nih.gov/books/ NBK560756/

Over the years, I have realized that God nurtured, admonished, guided, and guarded me, especially since I became eligible for the "call" at age nineteen. I tried to escape the draft or selective service by attempting college twice until a "greetings" letter formally "invited" me to "join" the Vietnam War. It didn't become my demise; I had a supportive and encouraging helpmate beside me during the rough adjustment times (*friendly fires* and *high-risk behaviors*) in a soldier's life. Now with opened eyes, God's strong hand was there all along.

Reading a newly published book about Ulysses S. Grant by Bret Baier reminded me that one of the best-known commanders in the American Civil War (second only to General Robert E. Lee) was General Thomas Jonathan "Stonewall" Jackson. Baier reported that Jackson suffered and died from friendly fire from Confederate comrades called "pickets." [1] The general lost his left arm to amputation; weakened by his wounds, he died of pneumonia eight days later. [2]

High-risk behaviors plagued Grant. He was known to be addicted to alcohol throughout his life (his close associates and family argued to the contrary). He and his close friend in war, General William Tecumseh Sherman, notorious for his destruction of Atlanta and "March to the Sea," was often called separately a drunk and crazy. Grant and Sherman's infrequent but unusual, uncharacteristic behavior were publicized for news' sake early in their careers. This aberrant conduct seemed to plague their aggressive war triumphs and brought their stability into question. Baier's book did not outright defend the two great generals or their behavior. Still, it recalled that their cynics told stories, never forgetting their early questionable behaviors: Grant's drinking excessively and Sherman's mental breakdown. Sherman reminded Julia, Grant's wife, that her husband would be slammed in the press as a coward, a drunk, a cheat, and more when he ran for president. Apparently, she got used to it.

Spiritually, we have our own friendly fire and high-risk behaviors that will bring us down to apparent helplessness or even a mortal death. Both spiritual and physical destruction is at hand when help and care are shunned and denied. These two great civil war generals had their challenges, either submitting to or overcoming their past; our healing and protection are found in the hope and grace only offered by the Lord.

"Too hard, can't continue, not worth it, going to give up, life was better on the outside," were all whining and thoughts of desperation in basic training in May 1968. Foot blisters, weaknesses exposed, awkwardness and embarrassment, in that small world of the training platoon of forty men conscripted by draft or court-ordered and "lifers" because we enlisted. I was pinned (i.e., appointed) as their acting platoon sergeant because of my boasting (*high-risk behavior*) about attending ROTC in college (barely a semester). I thought, "what did I get myself into?"

Calling my wife as often as possible and attending chapel on Sundays provided solace until I returned to the barracks. I lost my stripes when I started wearing flip-flops for my severe case of blisters. My drill sergeant asked how I could lead and not set the example (*friendly fire*). He removed me from my private cadre room and, to my fate, placed me in the center bunk, where my fellow soldiers chided me and were delighted in my demise. I thought I had been separated from these confrontational recalcitrants (i.e., subordinates); I now felt their hate. There would be the price to pay for my weak and failed leadership, as one who had no more tenure in the Army than they had.

A contemporary secular song titled "Friendly Fires" implores us to consider the injuries of friendly fires. The vocalist shares with his admirer that the past follows him like "ghosts" from somewhere down the road. He comments that he refuses to live in fear of getting close to someone because "friendly fires" always hurt the greatest. The lover doubles down again that he will not give his heart to someone who wouldn't give theirs in return because the friendly fires always hurt the "most." [3]

IN LIFE, WE FACE GIANTS OF THE PRESENT AND INDIVIDUAL BATTLES FROM STRUGGLES OF THE PAST

We are often afraid to take a risk because we've been hurt by presumed friends before and don't want to be hurt again (*friendly fire*). To overcome this fear takes courage, strength, and something more potent than heartfelt desire. It takes God's spiritual motivation to transform a relationship and life's behavior. We can see it in Scripture from another great war general, David. He kept thinking, "Someday Saul is going to get me. The best thing I can do is escape to the Philistines. Then Saul will stop hunting for me in Israelite territory, and I will finally be safe" (1 Samuel 27:1). David's plight with Saul caused him to be bitter in spirit.

Fear or pessimism can be a huge shot that wounds us spiritually and physically, causing us to take things into our own hands (*friendly fire*). We feel emotionally drained and downcast and are not always on top of our game. Sometimes we face the giants of our times and individual battles in life. We may also become wounded by the pandemic, disease, and illness, family dysfunction, job loss, or personal failures. Eventually, we may come to our wit's end in despair and dread (*high-risk behaviors*).

We need strength and refreshment during these times, where we are better in commitment, might, and outlook. We want to see a vision or path forward beyond our present heartfelt fears and compassion fatigues. Joe Barnett says, "Hope is the vaccine that inoculates us against the virus of despair." [4] Gene Shelburne writes, "The antidote for fear is the presence of God." [5] He also reminds us,

> That from beginning to end the Bible tells us that the antidote for fear is faith. Faith in a God greater than anything or anybody who might harm us. Faith in a God who keeps count of the hairs of our head. Faith in a God whose presence makes us able to confront any foe. [6]

Hope and faith are two of our tactical weapons and eternal spiritual medications for our self-imposed high-risk behaviors, our self-inflicted or friendly fire arrows which mortally wound us.

As Christian soldiers who sing the words of the song "We Have an Anchor," [7] do we mean it? We picture a distressed ship tossed, strained, billowing, and torn by the waves. We envision how our lives resemble this when traveling through the storms of strife, fraught with stress and choking pressures, temptations that try our faith and perseverance.

Will our faith keep us secure in those storms of life, or will we find our anchor drifting away?

We come to believe it by trusting and placing a secure hope in the Lord's might, not our own. Singing and listening to words founded in truth, not human insight, seems good and right. This faith leads us to join the chorus of that great song, knowing that our anchor keeps our soul steadfast and secure while fastened and grounded firmly and deeply in the Savior's love for us. Praise God!

Here is the rest of the story regarding David's plight with Saul and his bitter spirit. We find a pinnacle moment in the situation that we can cherish from a great warrior and leader of another militia, the army of Israel. "David was now in great danger because all his men were very bitter about losing their sons and daughters, and they began to talk of stoning him. But David found strength in the LORD his God" (1 Samuel 30:6).

Memories of what things were like before basic training with visions of the end kept me going. Glimmers of hope emerged from the depths of the darkest valley and began to raise my spirits. When my wounds healed, I grew stronger physically and mentally, counting down the days to graduation, achieving a top company record as an expert marksman, and completing survival in a harsh jungle-like Vietnam that Fort Polk could provide.

I also had an above-satisfactory PT score and would graduate from basic combat training. My graduation reward was surprising; I received orders for follow-on instruction in our final basic training formation. I was shocked to learn that I was on the pathway to the next training I was promised. A peripety (i.e., a sudden or unexpected reversal of circumstances or situation) moment! I wasn't going to "Tiger Land" or North Fort. In my intense training, we all had been somewhat brainwashed that we were heading there for jungle training, then going to Vietnam (*friendly fire*).

DAVID FOUND STRENGTH IN THE LORD HIS GOD

At another time, when David seemed to be at rock bottom in his life, he wrote:

> I love you, Lord; you are my strength. The Lord is my rock, my fortress, and my savior; my God is my rock, in whom I find protection. He is my shield, the power that saves me, and my place of safety. I called on the Lord, who is worthy of praise, and he saved me from my enemies. (Psalm 18:1-3)

David sought the Lord as his strength and stronghold, his foundation of hope. Can we trust Him as David did?

Accompanied by my loving wife, I experienced several technical training schools and duty assignments, both challenging and demanding, in CONUS and OCONUS locations. Still, I was unsure of making the Army a career. The promotions were faster than usual, and the pay became better. I wondered if I might advance on a different track with my technical achievements and experience by becoming a warrant officer. I had received favorable recommendations, approved by the board, and waited for the Army's approval.

After a long-anticipated wait, I was approved for promotion to warrant officer, but the Department of the Army (DA) would soon close that specialty. Shot down! *(friendly fire)* However, the Army opened another occupational field, and the review board approved me, but my experience didn't have the depth needed to qualify at DA. Thoughts began to convince us to consider an alternative to the Army.

Life is not always "Blue Skies and Rainbows," [8] as our kids have sung at youth camp. It's not all roses, lollipops, or teddy bears and lullabies. Eventually, we grow up and realize that life isn't what we were led to believe *(high-risk behaviors)*. Still, there is truth in that song if we recall the chorus that assures us that Jesus is alive and well today, making his home in our hearts—promising us with the firm assurance that we will never be alone again because He will never depart.

Life can have many temptations, selfish desires, and compelling feelings. It's filled with friends with commonsensical beliefs that appear harmless and controllable *(friendly fire)*.

In 1977, my wife's maternity nurse's husband and best friend, Ed Boyer, suggested Officer Candidate School (OCS). He volunteered to help me train, and if I would apply and get selected, I could make the deadline for being commissioned in under ten years and a waiver for my age of twenty-nine. In short, I was evaluated by a division-level board of field-grade officers and received initial approval. While stationed in Germany, I was selected by the commissioning group at the Department of the Army and trained for six months by running and playing racket ball three nights a week at V (5th) Corps Headquarters, where Ed worked on the commanding general's staff. I then returned stateside with my wife and son of four months to attend OCS. Two unsuccessful attempts earlier to carry a baby long-term had occurred in the past ten years; our third try resulted in a fine baby boy, born in Frankfurt, West Germany *(friendly fire)*. Praise God!

DON'T BE SELFISH WITH WHAT THE LORD HAS GIVEN US. SPIRITUAL STRENGTH IS FOUND IN HIS GRACE.

David found spiritual strength in the Lord and recovered everything according to 1 Samuel 30:18-19. But when faced with his troops' rationale and attempted persuasion, David experienced *friendly fire*. We read:

> Then David returned to the brook Besor and met up with the 200 men who had been left behind because they were too exhausted to go with him. They went out to meet David and his men, and David greeted them joyfully. But some evil troublemakers among David's men said, 'They didn't go with us, so they can't have any of the plunder we recovered. Give them their wives and children and tell them to be gone.' But David said, 'No, my brothers! Don't be selfish with what the LORD has given us. He has kept us safe and helped us defeat the band of raiders that attacked us. Who will listen when you talk like this? We share and share alike—those who go to battle and those who guard the equipment.' (1 Samuel 30:21-24)

David told his men they had the wrong idea. They were not to be selfish with the generous bounty the Lord had given. As with David, our spiritual strength is in His grace. Isn't that where we can find our authentic strength? So, don't take the credit. It may appear that it was because of what you did. But if your faith and power are in the Lord, then the credit belongs to Him.

Officer Candidate School was grueling both physically and mentally. Still, the challenges were achievable, as I relied on my experiences, vision, knowledge, and seeing what lay beyond the fourteen weeks of basic infantry officer candidate course. Also, a big help was the weekly chapel services, where I could sit with my wife and near-year-old son and sing in the choir at early service. Additionally, a weekly visit from her in the company day room was a high point. Of course, I had to work off demerits (*friendly fires*), perform dismounted drilling, and tolerate cold winter training at Fort Benning, Georgia; however, the prize we all envisioned was pinning on the "butter bar" of a Second Lieutenant (2LT).

A song comes to mind that we used to begin our worship services is called "Doxology" (*aka*, "Praise God for Whom All Blessings Flow"). [9] Now, with the Lord, a dear friend taught me to praise Him in everything. He said more than once when I re-counted a seeming coincidence, "thank your Lord, the Lord is blessing you" for this or that. Even the simple things like being late for an event: all traffic lights were green, an empty parking spot awaited me in front of the building, and we were on time. He said, "the Lord is blessing you, Alan."

Need more reminders? A bounty of powerful verses can strengthen us in His grace and hope. Here are a few:

- "The Lord gives his people strength. The Lord blesses them with peace" (Psalm 29:11).

- "Timothy, my dear son, be strong through the grace that God gives you in Christ Jesus" (2 Timothy 2:1).

- "He gives power to the weak and strength to the powerless. Even youths will become weak and tired, and young men will fall in exhaustion. But those who trust in the LORD will find new strength. They will soar high on wings like eagles. They will run and not grow weary. They will walk and not faint" (Isaiah 40:29-31).

After training and commissioning, the assignments were very demanding. Being an older, seasoned Lieutenant, I was made the detachment commander at Fort Sill, Oklahoma, where I had to make hard leadership choices for mission and discipline. Based on my leadership training, good counsel, faith, and perseverance, my decisions were upheld, and I was given more responsibility. When returning to Germany a second time to command a large missile maintenance company in the 3rd Armored Division, more equipment, troop responsibility, mission, and welfare decisions were assumed.

Weekly church services and ministry positions gave me a change of focus beyond military matters to a yielding grace and faith to be demonstrated. Reliable NCOs, officers, and a competent and technically savvy team of soldiers made the company mission successful. Some soldiers challenged my view of discipline in some occurrences, but they reservedly accepted it. Some of my commanders thought I was too compassionate (*friendly fires*), and punishment should have been much more severe. I felt my punishments were justified to repay the wrong done rather than ruining a life. So, I stood by my decisions.

WE MUST PURSUE THE LORD'S STRENGTH

There is more to knowing the truth and God's wisdom, which He has freely given us; we must also pursue His strength. When days are unmerciful, and we are intimidated and discouraged, the Lord will be there for us with a strong arm and encouragement. Persevering through self-control and determination might be what we feel is needed but by pursuing our strength in the Lord, we pray and wait on the Lord's blessings of grace, mercy, and His mighty hand to accomplish great things. Take confidence in these verses:

- "But LORD, be merciful to us, for we have waited for you. Be our strong arm each day and our salvation in times of trouble" (Isaiah 33:2).

- "They were just trying to intimidate us, imagining that they could discourage us and stop the work. So, I continued the work with even greater determination" (Nehemiah 6:9).

After twenty years, my choice to retire from the Army was not wholly mine. My record was clean, I achieved my goals for advancement, and my awards were even meritorious. Still, one former evaluation report indicated a lack of good judgment for discipline. Therefore, I wasn't readily promotable. My superiors recommended hanging in there, but my faith suggested I go another way (*friendly fire*). I chose to take my growth in perseverance and mission accomplishments to the civilian industry arena.

For thirty years following the military, I was successful in management, leading a great group of people who contributed much despite their journeys through their friendly fires and high-risk behaviors. I am thankful they seemed to be influenced by my dynamic behaviors and the spirituality God developed in my life.

DEFEAT THE GIANTS OF DELAY, DISCOURAGEMENT, DISAPPROVAL, AND DOUBT.

To summarize this life story, Rick Warren provides four godly principles that we can use to give us hope in defense of the spiritual battles against the forces of friendly fire and our high-risk behaviors. I faced many of these same problems in the military that we all continually face throughout life. I believe they are trustworthy and memorable. Start by doing the four things David did to defeat the giants of delay, discouragement, disapproval, and doubt in his life, all of which are self-inflicted and deny the power of Jesus Christ our Savior.

REMEMBER HOW GOD HELPED YOU IN THE PAST

David said in 1 Samuel 17:37, "The LORD who rescued me from the claws of the lion and the bear will rescue me from this Philistine!"

Saul finally consented. "All right, go ahead," he said. "And may the LORD be with you!"

USE THE TOOLS GOD HAS GIVEN YOU IN THE PRESENT

God provided David with tools that tapped into his strengths:

Then Saul gave David his armor ... 'I can't go in these,' he protested to Saul. 'I'm not used to them.' So, David took them off again. He picked up five smooth stones from a stream and put them into his shepherd's bag. Then, armed only with his shepherd's staff and sling, he started across the valley to fight the Philistine" (1 Samuel 17:38-40).

IGNORE THE DREAM BUSTERS

Later in life, when others were speaking against him, David had to encourage himself in the Lord. He "was now in great danger because all his men were very bitter about losing their sons and daughters, and they began to talk of stoning him. But David found strength in the LORD his God" (1 Samuel 30:6).

EXPECT GOD TO HELP YOU FOR HIS GLORY

David stormed the battlefield, shouting:

You come to me with sword, spear, and javelin, but I come to you in the name of the LORD of Heaven's Armies—the God of the armies of Israel, whom you have defied. Today the LORD will conquer you, and I will kill you and cut off your head. And then I will give the dead bodies of your men to the birds and wild animals, and the whole world will know that there is a God in Israel!" (1 Samuel 17:45-46)

God can use anyone who trusts and expects Him to—not because of who you are but because of who He is. [10]

Years after military retirement and on many occasions, I recalled how things were dealt with, actions taken, and how their consequences played out. I am now confident and happy that while I acted on *high-risk behaviors* and dealt with *friendly fire*, I recalled my past help, using the tools I acquired, ignored the dream busters, and praised God for His strong hand, knowing it was to His glory. My "ghosts" have become my strength. Thirty years later, my life's career has included being a pastoral caregiver, counselor, and chaplain for veterans. I continue to press on to help others enable their grace-filled life to be a light for the Lord's glory and by praising His promises.

In conclusion, regarding Grant and Sherman, I don't know their heart or relationship with the Lord during that awful history of the American Civil War. Still, I am confident many mothers, fathers, and families of the divided nation were on their knees petitioning for the conflict and destruction to be over. May we glorify the Lord that the surrender at Appomattox took place on April 9, 1865. As for me, the *spiritual friendly fires* and *high-risk behaviors* have taught me to rely on the strength of my Lord and not be lost or feel unrewarded through my weaknesses when wounded spiritually.

ALAN LANGFORD, U.S. Army, Retired

MOSs: (Enlisted) Nike Hercules Fire Control Crewman/Maintenance Mechanic/Calibration Specialist. (Officer) Ordnance Missile Materiel Management/Procurement Management, Space Activities.

EMAIL: alanlangfordhsv@gmail.com

EDITOR'S NOTE: Alan has many years of experience in pastoral care as a church shepherd/elder and as a hospital chaplain. He obtained post-military training from Light University, attaining the International Board of Christian and Pastoral Counseling credential of Board Certified Pastoral Counselor. Alan is also a board-certified Mental Health Coach.

ENDNOTES:

1 Bret Baier, *To Rescue the Republic, Ulysses S. Grant, the Fragile Union, and the Crisis of 1876.* (Worthington, OH: Custom House, 2021), np.

2 *Stonewall Jackson.* https://en.wikipedia.org/wiki/Stonewall_Jackson

3 *Friendly Fires.* https://www.azlyrics.com/lyrics/garethemery/friendlyfires.html

4 *Three Flawed Feuds.* http://www.christianappeal.com/issues/2021/ca_november_2021.pdf

5 Gene Shelburne, *The God Who Puts Us Back Together* (Joplin, MO: College Press Publishing Company, 1997), 48.

6 Shelburne, *The God Who Puts Us Back Together*, 47.

7 *We Have an Anchor.* https://hymnary.org/text/will_your_anchor_hold_in_the_storms_of_l

8 *Blue Skies And Rainbows.* https://www.rjstevensmusic.com/product/blue-skies-and-rainbows/

9 *Doxology.* https://amazinghymns.com/doxology-praise-god-from-whom-all-blessings-flow/

10 *Four Steps to Defeat Your Giants.* https://pastorrick.com/four-steps-to-defeat-your-giants/

CHAPTER 5
Spiritual Combat Casualty Care: Bloody Bunny

August 19, 2004, commenced like any other day while deployed to the Al Anbar Province of Iraq. It was a beautiful morning; temperatures hovered in the low to mid-90s. I had just finished breakfast and sat in front of our barracks in Camp Fallujah, waiting to begin my day. I had not intended to go outside the wire (i.e., off base) to get some company medical administrative things done. A Marine Corps patrol was walking toward their Humvees en route to Al Zanta to meet with the village sheik. They were returning weapons confiscated on the initial push into Fallujah (adult males of each home in the village were to have a means of self-defense).

As the Company Corpsman (Senior Navy Hospital Corpsman) of my Marine Rifle Company (aka Devil Doc), I was not required to participate in patrol. However, I had already been on over fifty combat missions with various squads and platoons. That day the patrol leader crossed my path, and I asked to go with them. Another corpsman was already assigned for this patrol, but something deep inside me said they needed an extra set of medical hands. The patrol leader looked at me and said, "Grab your gear Doc." When I arrived at the staging area with my combat kit, including my service weapon and medical bag, I started to get into the lead vehicle (I routinely rode with the patrol leader). The truck commander looked at me and said, "There's no room Doc; get in the third truck." When I arrived at the vehicle, I noticed it was a mortar truck. There were four cans of 60 mm mortar rounds, two mortar tubes, two cans of high explosives, and two cans of white phosphorus rounds on board. "This cannot be right!" I wondered if this might be a bad day traveling in a combat area, sitting on two cans of high explosive mortar rounds! Once we crossed the LOD or "line of departure" – "a phased line crossed at a prescribed time by troops initiating an offensive operation" [1] – it began as any other contact patrol.

We were on high alert with our weapon systems locked and loaded facing outboard or outward. I just sat in the middle of the troop compartment surrounded by America's best, armed with my 9mm service weapon. We passed over the main surface road connecting Al Tikrit, the home of Saddam Hussein, with Baghdad and proceeded to a secondary road that ran along an irrigation ditch. As we crossed the dirt bridge over the irrigation ditch, I noticed the pump station beside the central irrigation canal had recently been destroyed by terrorists operating in the area. Traveling northwest on this route headed toward Al Zanta, it was getting hotter, and our level of alertness only amplified with the knowledge of where we were going and area threats. The village where we were going was a known supporter of Saddam Hussein. We parked our vehicles in a defensive posture and dismounted upon arrival. Our patrol commander, along with several other Marines, approached some of the male members of the village and asked where the sheik was. They told us he was not there, which was strange as they knew we were coming; they knew the purpose of our visit, and it was the sheik's job to meet with us. Returning weapons or giving funds to the village went through the sheik, yet he was not there. After further conversation with the village males, we returned to our vehicles for the trip back to the base.

My vehicle moved first in the line back along the canal road. When we got to the pump station area, we stopped just before our left-hand turn to await the patrol commander's vehicle to follow him back to the base. At this time, I noticed a young Iraqi male raking straw in a field to my right. I exited my vehicle and retrieved a liter bottle of water and an MRE to take to the young man. Through my rudimentary knowledge of Arabic and our commonality as farmers, I communicated basic thoughts and put our minds at ease. After a few minutes, I returned to the vehicle and waited. Our commander, followed by another vehicle, appeared and took the lead. We returned to the number three position in the patrol order. The first two vehicles crossed a dirt bridge across the canal, and as we approached our turn to cross the bridge, I heard and saw one of the largest explosions I had yet to see in-country. Our driver accelerated across the bridge, made a left-hand turn, and assumed a right-side overwatch position atop a berm to our right for security, overlooking a large field where Iraqi men were on a tractor. I then grabbed my medical kit and exited the vehicle, running to where the first vehicle was supposed to be.

When I got closer, I realized it wasn't *where* it should have been; it had been pushed into the water-filled ditch by what I later learned was an IED, made from two 155 mm artillery rounds and an 81 mm mortar round. Upon arrival, I noticed the other corpsman was already in the troop compartment, rendering aid to the wounded. I stepped into the troop compartment and made my way to the front of the vehicle, where I noticed one Marine in the passenger seat slumped over the console and the driver unconscious in chest-deep water. One of our Lance Corporals and I pulled the driver out of the water, and I began to reach for the Marine in the passenger seat. As I reached for his belt, a Marine said, "Doc, he's gone!" I then turned my attention to the other wounded Marines: one of our Captains had shrapnel and blast wounds to his face and a Lance Corporal with severe injuries to his left arm. The other corpsman was rendering aid as I assisted him in applying a tourniquet made from my belt to the Marine with the wounded left arm and extracted the injured Captain from the vehicle onto the road. I bandaged his wounds as best I could and ensured that he was conscious and alive. As this all was happening, the other Marines in the patrol had already set up a 360° defensive posture awaiting an ambush. They also called our QRF (Quick Reaction Force) on standby aboard Camp Fallujah. Once the other corpsman and I had stabilized the most seriously wounded and bandaged the lesser wounded Marines, we loaded them into another vehicle to ride to the base and Bravo Surgical Company (e.g., Navy field treatment facility). The QRF arrived and escorted us back. Flash forward about thirty minutes to an hour ahead. After I had gone into Bravo Surgical to assist in any way I could with the two seriously wounded Marines, I went back outside to the refrigerated Connex box used as a makeshift morgue. A few Marines and I went into the Connex box, and by this time, the adrenaline had worn off, and the realization of what had just happened hit me incredibly hard.

Marine Corporal Brad McCormick from Allons, Tennessee, had given his last full measure of devotion to his God, his Corps, and his country. I then walked over to a Jersey barrier (i.e., a modular concrete or plastic wall employed to separate lanes of traffic), sat down, and began to weep uncontrollably. Throughout my career, I had lived with the self-imposed personal responsibility of not allowing any Marine to die on my watch when I had the opportunity to save his life. Navy Hospital Corpsmen assigned to a Fleet Marine Force unit live with the moniker "Death Cheater." Nevertheless, I felt personally responsible and cheated not to have had the opportunity to save Brad's life. Not cheated in a selfish way, but due to the terrorists' actions who placed the IED on the canal road before our being there that day. Brad was not the first Marine I had lost. I had a tragic event occur before we left Camp Pendleton, California, in February of that same year involving a Marine assigned to Division Schools. He perished as I worked to save him from a Humvee rollover accident on our battalion's convoy course.

Consequently, my mental, emotional, and spiritual struggle over the past seventeen years included questioning my belief structure regarding a loving and just God. Many servicemen and women struggle daily with similar thoughts and emotions, particularly those serving in combat arms. Why would a brother or sister die while I have to live? This personal struggle is not a self-centered thought process, however. It is more to the point of "why me?" or "why him!" The cliché "it is not for me reason why" doesn't apply here! It goes well beyond that and deep into the human psyche. The physical, mental, emotional, and spiritual trauma of dealing with death, particularly on the battlefield, is a complicated and painful phenomenon. I never had to fire my weapon in anger while on deployment. I received the Combat Action Ribbon for actions taken while part of a mortar team supporting combat action when an RPG round passed over my head and actions taken on this particular fateful day. However, the trauma of witnessing the death and dismemberment of several of my warrior brothers, both in combat and as the result of self-harm back home, has left an invisible scar that I must carry for the rest of my life. Transitioning to civilian life has been a particularly rough, painstakingly difficult, and personally damaging path for my family and friends.

Jesus' disciples asked Him why they could not cast out an evil spirit from a boy who suffered greatly from it. Jesus straightforwardly replied, "Because of your little faith. For truly, I say to you, if you have faith like a grain of mustard seed, you will say to this mountain, 'Move from here to there,' and it will move, and nothing will be impossible for you'" (Matthew 17:14ff). We have this one everlasting hope for all the anxiety and stressful life in the military. God is with His people. He has charged His angels to watch over us, protect us, and comfort us! He is there for all the times of fear, danger, and loss! Truthfully, many times during my spiritual journey, I have questioned my faith and all it entails. I have peered into the darkness and only seen the night despite my upbringing as a church elder's son and my loving, Christian mother. I grew up in the church and was baptized for the remission of my sins at twelve years old. I graduated from a Christian high school in St. Louis and a Christian university in Nashville, then married a Christian woman, fellowshipped with good Christian people, and went to church services often. Yet, I have had many times of doubt and insecurity when put to the test. I am sure many of you reading these words can relate! In the final analysis, I understand and appreciate that I still have "this living hope" (1 Peter 1:3).

When trials come (and they will), dangers abound, chaos and death are all around; whom do *you* trust? Who do *you* go to for shelter and comfort? The Lord of all creation (Hebrews 1:10-12) is our fortress (Psalms 18:2). The one thing I looked forward to when on a combat patrol (besides the men who were with me to protect and support me) was returning to base—our "fortress." It was a place of relative safety—where I could re-energize, rest, and find nutrition for my body. Our God is that spiritual fortress, that base. He is where we can go when facing the trauma of life's battlefields. With the uncertainty and chaos of time "outside the wire," we have confidence and calm "inside the wire" where God is.

I GOT YOUR SIX!

In seeking to tempt Jesus in various ways, Satan understood that God would protect His Son if He only jumped from the temple's pinnacle. "For it is written, 'He will command His angels concerning you to guard you'" (Luke 4:10). While Jesus didn't give into the devil's wily ways, the fact remains that angels are heavenly beings who are "ministering spirits sent out to serve for the sake of those who are to inherit salvation (Hebrews 1:14). These guardian angels, both seen and unseen, are spiritual protectors by which we can live our day-to-day existence without the worry and care of the constant threat.

Who are your "angels"? In the infantry, particularly while on patrol, we had "guardian angels." These Marines would be on our flanks (sides), deep in the bush or away from our formation, who would alert and protect us from attack. In addition, we had a "point man," a Marine who would lead the patrol to warn us of an enemy coming toward us; we also had a Marine in the rear of our formation. Some refer to this man as the "Tail-End Charlie," who would help ensure no enemy came from behind us. Thus, we had a 360-degree bubble of protection, and therefore, they were our "angels." In combat, we would also have aerial security or close air support (CAS). These fixed and/or rotary-wing aircraft were on station to close in on the enemy at a moment's notice if we found ourselves in heavy enemy contact. These assets, along with artillery, mortars, and drone flights, provided us with a real sense of protection in a very chaotic and highly volatile area.

In the military, 'got your six' means 'I've got your back.' The saying originated with World War I fighter pilots referencing the rear of an airplane as the six o'clock position. If you picture yourself at the center of a clock face, the area directly in front of you is twelve o'clock. Six o'clock is what lies behind you. On a battlefield, your 'six' is the most vulnerable. So, when someone tells you that they've 'got your six,' it means they're watching your back. By extension, that person expects you to have their back as well. 'Got your six' is now a ubiquitous term in the military that also highlights the way military members look out for each other. [2]

I believe these special servants are law enforcement officers, fire, other emergency workers, our families, friends, fellow Christians, and so forth. One of my favorite passages in the Bible that describe angelic protection is 2 Kings 6:14-17. In this story, the king of modern-day Syria sent a massive army to Dothan to capture the prophet, Elisha. When his servant went outside one morning and saw the mighty army surrounding them, he was frightened! Elisha said, "Do not be afraid, for those who are with us are more than those who are with them" (2 Kings 6:16; cf. 1 John 4:4). Seeing his servant's fear, Elisha asked God to "open his [i.e., servant's] eyes that he can see." When God did as Elisha asked, his servant saw a massive angelic army surrounding the warriors the Syrian king had sent. So, I ask again: who are *your* "angels"? In whom do *you* trust? Who is *your* fortress? Where does *your* strength come from? With this, the question remains: "If God is for us, who can stand against us?" (Romans 8:31).

You may be wondering about the subtitle for this chapter, *Bloody Bunny*. Part of the patrol we were on that day when my friend's (Corporal Brad McCormick) life ended was to support the Civil Affairs Group (CAG) and deliver stuffed animals to the children of the Iraqi village we were visiting. With the sheik's absence that day, the toys were not delivered and were in the back of the attacked Humvee. One of the CAG photographers took a picture of the aftermath that burned into my brain. It was a stuffed bunny covered in the precious blood of one of our warriors. That tragic event showed me that even the best intentions could have negative outcomes.

In summation, this event brings me back to the initial discussion about fear where, in Isaiah 41:10, God said, "Fear not, for I am with you; be not dismayed, for I am your God; I will strengthen you, I will help you, I will uphold you with my righteous right hand." If you or a loved one suffers from mental or emotional trouble related to combat or other service-related trauma, please reach out! The bravery shown during military service doesn't end afterward. There are numerous support networks, both private and through the government. I have sought help from Christian counselors, civilian therapists, the Vet Center (Readjustment Counseling), and the Veteran Affairs Administration (I have also been under the care of the VA's Mental Health teams since 2018). Combined with my relatives' love and support, including family, friends, and fellow Christians, I am doing much better than before. However, all the combined help, my faith, and trust in the Lord cannot entirely keep the demons away by my efforts alone. I must take time and study God's Word, pray, and dedicate time for self-care in my already hectic and busy life. *I encourage you to do the same.*

ERIC OWENS, U.S. Navy Reserve (Fleet Marine Force), Retired
RATING: Combat Hospital Corpsman / Senior Medical Specialist
EMAIL: doc.owens@comcast.net

EDITOR'S NOTE: Eric is Associate Head Athletic Trainer at Tennessee State University and has a Master's in Education from Lipscomb University.

ENDNOTES:

1 *Line of Departure*. https://www.globalsecurity.org/military/library/policy/army/fm/3-90/ch3.htm#par4-9

2 *Got your back*. https://wgy6.org/

CHAPTER 6

Spiritual Echelons of Care

All Scripture references are from the New American Standard Bible.

After basic combat training, my initial AIT instruction was the Army's Combat Medic Course at Fort Sam Houston in San Antonio, Texas. I was an 18-year-old country boy from a small farm town in upstate New York. I knew a "medic" was the guy with the Red Cross armband who patched you up on the battlefield, carried you off, and gave you morphine to numb the pain. I grew up watching "M.A.S.H" (short for Mobile Army Surgical Hospital) and had seen my share of war movies. Not that John Rambo ever needed a medic or morphine! (He stitched his own wounds—more on that later.) The combat medic training was a pre-requisite to the Army's Orthopedic Specialist Course held at the former Fitzsimmons Army Medical Center (FAMC) in Aurora, Colorado.

While there, I met Mr. Ulysses Stanley, or "Stan," as everyone called him. He was the "Professor" for the orthopedic program. As it turned out, Stan was a retired soldier who served as a combat medic and flew into hot LZs or landing zones in a Huey helicopter to extract physically wounded warriors (which is not to say they didn't suffer mentally and emotionally but did later). The landing pad for the medevac helos was directly across the street from the orthopedic trauma unit. Recounting when choppers would come in, Stan would put his arm out and say, "Look, guys! I still get chills!" He was legit and had plenty of real-world experience to share; his story about patching all the bullet holes in the chopper with beer cans and spraying them with olive drab paint still blows my mind. He said he used to marvel that (1) he didn't get hit and (2) the chopper still flew, having been shot up so much.

At FAMC, in July of 1986, I met the author of chapter seven of this book, *Spiritual Battle Scars*, Mel Caraway (who also co-authored *Spiritual Battle Rattle: God's Army*; he was the NCOIC or boss of the Orthopedic Department. He was integral in the hands-on phase of my early orthopedic training and later, as a young private, assigned to "Fitz," as we called it, after graduation. Mel was a walking encyclopedia of medical and orthopedic knowledge to share, as you'd expect from any senior enlisted soldier. He was also a deacon in his church in Denver. Little did I know that Mel would become the spiritual medic God sent to pull me out of the world and into His church. This began the spiritual process of revealing a whole new classification of wounds and required treatments, leading me to this chapter's theme. (If you haven't, I highly encourage you to read the book *Spiritual Battle Rattle: God's Armor*. It is beyond this scope, but you will discover that most spiritual wounds requiring a spiritual combat medic are directly tied to not putting on the whole armor of God and standing firm in it.)

SPIRITUAL MEDICS – SAVING SPIRITUAL LIVES

The United States Army's website defines the role of combat medics in the following manner:

> As a Combat Medic Specialist, you'll administer emergency medical care in the field in both combat and humanitarian situations. You'll serve as a *first responder* and triage illnesses and injuries to *save lives*. You'll also *train other Soldiers* in lifesaver/first responder courses" (emphasis mine, *pf*). [1]

Training for this enlisted position involves the initial ten weeks of BCT (basic combat training), followed by sixteen weeks of AIT. I want to highlight two aspects of this role as they perfectly define the "spiritual medic" role. They are to "save lives" and "train other soldiers" in a spiritual sense. While these two missions are separate, they both are vitally essential to the health of God's Army, the church. Foremost is the call "to save lives" as a "first responder … in the field in … combat." God has commissioned His Army for this mission with clear standing orders as spelled out in Matthew 28:18-20,

> And Jesus came up and spoke to them, saying, 'All authority in heaven and on earth has been given to Me. Go, therefore, and make disciples of all the nations, baptizing them in the name of the Father and the Son and the Holy Spirit, teaching them to follow all that I commanded you; and behold, I am with you always, to the end of the age.'

Jesus said in Luke 19:10, "For the Son of Man has come to seek and to save that which was lost." We will eventually succumb to battle wounds that God calls sin in spiritual terms. The book of Romans records: "as it is written: 'THERE IS NO RIGHTEOUS PERSON, NOT EVEN ONE' ... for all have sinned and fall short of the glory of God" (3:10, 23). All of humanity is involved in this spiritual battle with sin! (some eight billion people by the last count.) The tragedy is that most people have no idea they're in a fight for their lives and eternal souls. They have been drafted into service for the enemy, alive physically, consciously, but spiritually killed-in-action or missing-in-action by self-inflicted wounds. Satan has deceived them into believing lies such as "finding your own truth is the highest calling in life" and "your identity is whatever you choose it to be." These are more philosophical lies. Satan's biggest lie? He (the devil) simply does not exist, nor does God. And even if God does exist, He is a God of love and made you who you are; He would *never* send anyone to hell, so go ahead, "You do you!"

As spiritual medics or first responders, we have a specific command, a clear mission consisting of four elements per Matthew 28:19-20. Our *first duty* is to "go." As Christians, we recognize that what is seen in the physical world extends to the unseen battle in the spiritual realm (cf. Ephesians 6:12). God created you for a higher purpose than simply pleasing yourself. Your spiritual mission is to engage in this unseen fight to save souls—yours and others. "For the love of

Christ controls us, having concluded this, that one died for all, therefore all died; and He died for all, so that those who live would no longer live for themselves, but for Him who died and rose on their behalf" (2 Corinthians 5:14-15).

Our *second duty* as spiritual medics or first responders is to "make disciples." This is where your life finds meaning. It is an ongoing process of growth and development, your own and others. 2 Corinthians 5:20 says, "Therefore, we are ambassadors for Christ, as though God were making an appeal through us; we beg you on behalf of Christ, be reconciled to God." Your spiritual identity and purpose are found here as God's chosen representative. (Duties *three* and *four* are subsets in number *two* and answer the "how" of the Lord's command to "make disciples.")

The additional duty of a spiritual medic extends to *"baptizing them"* (I will explain number *four* below). As a disciple of Jesus, He commissions you to go into the battlefield of spiritual combat and save lives by making disciples or Jesus-followers. It is by the mode of baptism (e.g., immersion or submersion) that spiritual lives are saved through the forgiveness of sins. The blood of Christ heals those self-inflicted sin wounds that lead to death. Colossians 2:11-13 states,

> In Him you were also circumcised with a circumcision performed without hands, in the removal of the body of the flesh by the circumcision of Christ, having been buried with Him in baptism, in which you were also raised with Him through faith in the working

of God, who raised Him from the dead. And when you were dead in your wrongdoings and the uncircumcision of your flesh, He made you alive together with Him, having forgiven us all our wrongdoings.

SPIRITUAL MEDICS – TRAINING OTHER SOLDIERS

The *fourth duty* of spiritual medics is to "train other soldiers" and is reflected in the last part of the call, "teaching them to follow all that I commanded you" (Matthew 28:20a). Paul told Timothy, "The things which you have heard from me in the presence of many witnesses, entrust these to faithful people who will be able to teach others also" (2 Timothy 2:2). Below, I will simply illustrate the essential importance of this role and in the final section, I will describe how this looks in our congregation. Then more specifically, we will examine higher echelons or levels of care as needs arise.

All Christians hold the role and responsibilities of a spiritual medic. In medical terms, we are all physician extenders or assistants of the Great Physician. As Darren Crowden highlighted in the *Epilogue* of *Spiritual Battle Rattle: God's Armor*, we need to consider all the "one another" passages in Scripture. As the body of Christ, we are members of one another—that is, having an interrelationship with fellow Christians. In Ephesians 1:22-23, the apostle Paul states, "And He put all things in subjection under His feet and made Him head over all things to the church, which is His body, the fullness of Him who fills all in all." The church of our Lord Jesus Christ is a living organism. Coming from a medical background, I have always appreciated "anatomical" illustrations in Scripture. Paul's imagery in First Corinthians 12:12-27 is classic as he concludes, "Now you are Christ's body, and individually members of it."

I like to illustrate the church in the following way (it is simplistic, to be sure, but it works), so here goes. I am one *cell* in Christ's *body*. Along with my brothers and sisters, we are *tissue*. The local congregation is an *organ*. Regional assemblies (e.g., large cities, surrounding towns, counties, etc.) comprise organ *systems* and different body *parts*. Carry that out worldwide, and you have Christ's entire body. As with your physical body, the inherent health of Christ's spiritual body, His church, is directly linked to the health of *every* individual cell.

A tragedy of the church, in my experience, is the attitude of measuring our spiritual health only by the number of baptisms or conversions we have had (I've been guilty of this in my younger years and don't mean to broad-brush everyone). But how many have been rescued from the spiritual battlefield of the world only to become spiritually battle casualties due to little or no real further spiritual combat training? These Christian warriors were never equipped to face life's battles! In his book, *All In*, Mark Batterson says, "The problem with many Christians is they may have been saved for 20 years. But all they've done is live that first year over, 20 times." [2] All too often, it's not entirely their fault!

There is a reason the military calls its initial instruction "Basic Combat Training" – it is just the *beginning* of one's transformation. Hebrews 5:12-14 says,

> For though by this time you ought to be teachers, you have need again for someone to teach you the elementary principles of the actual words of God, and you have come to need milk and not solid food. For everyone who partakes only of milk is unacquainted with the word of righteousness, for he is an infant. But solid food is for the *mature, who because of practice have their senses trained to distinguish between good and evil."* (emphasis mine, *pf*)

Maturity is integral to Jesus' command to "make disciples." But as I mentioned above, sometimes we are tempted to think we've done that just because we studied with and baptized someone into Christ. We have helped make a disciple in one sense, which is paramount! Nonetheless, there is a "next step," and both are vitally important. Consider *hearing the gospel* (e.g., the good news of Jesus' death, burial, and resurrection; 1 Corinthians 15:1ff), *faith*, and *obedience* to God's commands as "basic combat training" with *baptism* (immersion) as your graduation. You have now been delivered from spiritual death into spiritual life (Colossians 1:13).

That "following step" (as mentioned above) launches you into a lifelong process of spiritual training that only ends when you leave your physical body behind (i.e., death). Spiritual instruction is the church's primary responsibility (your new spiritual family), which means you

and your soul. Continual training and growth occur corporately and individually. You may not yet be a spiritual drill instructor (DI), but you know enough to recruit new troops! (The person who trained you—your spiritual DI—can help you prepare them as you learn.)

The Army's training program takes a minimum of twenty-six weeks to prepare as a combat medic. At this point, you are equipped with the essential knowledge to perform your duty. Through the requisite time, training and experience, these courses are taught by experienced staff qualified to pass that knowledge on to others. Successfully completing the program doesn't mean you are now ready for your job, however. Receiving a "Go" at the various required skills assessment stations is a far cry from performing those skills in actual combat. There is a vast difference between triaging a practice or mock casualty scene and treating a soldier made up with moulage wounds compared to a true warrior who has their real guts spilled out or a limb blown off. When not involved in actual combat, a medic or corpsman is constantly training to maintain a high state of readiness. That is why first responders, nurses, and providers in all areas of healthcare and other skill professions, when questioned about their roles, say something like, "That is when your training just kicks in." I dare say many spiritual wounds that Christians receive can be avoided with the proper ongoing training required to maintain a high degree of readiness. Why? Because they are then better prepared to combat and be protected from those things which cause spiritual wounds. (Note that I did not say this training renders one bulletproof!)

Real growth and maturity come from doing or obeying God's word, which implies you indeed *heard* it. This understanding occurs in your mind and not in your ears. James says in 1:22-24,

> But prove yourselves doers of the word, and not just hearers who deceive themselves. For if anyone is a hearer of the word and not a doer, he is like a man who looks at his natural face in a mirror; for once he has looked at himself and gone away, he has immediately forgotten what kind of person he was.

Jesus often said to His audiences, "The one who has ears, let him hear" (Matthew 11:15). He wasn't talking about everyone in earshot! Tens of thousands heard Jesus's words; however, not all of them took it into their minds and hearts, pondered it, and were changed by it, resulting in a transformed life. That was Jesus' point.

SPIRITUAL MEDICS AND HIGHER ECHELONS OF CARE

In ministering the word, local congregations play a vital role. It is here that all spiritual warriors receive ongoing preventative care. And when wounded, they are triaged or sorted as needed to higher echelons of care. In our congregation, our overall emphasis is on "making disciples." There are several facets to this. The first component is *evangelism*. A person returns from the spiritual battlefield of the world through the lifesaving transfusion of Christ's blood. At this point, they have full access to all the spiritual healthcare and preventative medicine the church offers. Also mentioned above, this occurs both collectively and individually.

Hebrews 10:24-25 says, "Let's consider how to encourage one another in love and good deeds, not abandoning our own meeting together, as is the habit of some people, but encouraging one another; and all the more as you see the day drawing near." We are meant to gather together weekly and are commanded by God to do so! One of the vital healing elements of our regular assembly is encouragement: injecting courage into every soldier of Christ. When we meet, we see brothers and sisters struggling similarly (recall that we are members of one another, meaning that we belong to each other).

At any given time in life, we are all spiritually walking wounded (some not even walking). Every Sunday, God's Emergency Department (the church) is open to providing spiritual care (primary care and preventative medicine rolled into one). The specific "medics" providing primary care are Bible class teachers and preachers in this case. As you'd expect from your Family Medicine doc or any frontline care specialist, these individuals are responsible for "doing no harm." We trust they have studied and possess the skills and desire to communicate God's truths effectively. Paul challenged Timothy to 'be diligent … handling accurately the word of truth" (2 Timothy 2:15). James admonished, "Do not become teachers in large numbers, my brothers, since you know that we who are teachers will incur a stricter judgment" (3:1).

In this regard, caring for the body of Christ requires diligent study, copious prayer, and ongoing practice! The church is spiritually led and fed by the effective preaching and teaching of God's word under the watchful care of men called elders or overseers who shepherd or lead the church (cf. Acts 20:28; 1 Timothy 3:1ff; Titus 1:6ff). Proper spiritual nutrition could be a book on its own but know it is integral to one's spiritual health and healing just as it is physically! (cf. Matthew 4:4) It is also through this that the Holy Spirit, via God's word, can do His work in our lives, performing necessary procedures or surgeries which ultimately bring healing (cf. Hebrews 4:12 and James 1:21). Ephesians 4:11-15 tells us,

> And He [God] gave some as apostles, some as prophets, some as evangelists, some as pastors and teachers, for the equipping of the saints for the work of ministry, for the building up of the body of Christ; until we all attain to the unity of the faith, and of the knowledge of the Son of God, to a mature man, to the measure of the stature which belongs to the fullness of Christ. As a result, we are no longer to be children, tossed here and there by waves and carried about by every wind of doctrine, by the trickery of people, by craftiness in deceitful scheming; but speaking the truth in love, we are to grow up in all aspects into Him who is the head, that is, Christ.

We could examine other relevant passages, but Paul sums it up well here. Note the type of care rendered and the goal of that treatment when we assemble: "equipping, "building up," "attain to the unity of the faith," "knowledge of the Son of God," "mature," "no longer children." The New Living Translation says it another way: "We will no longer be immature like children. We won't be tossed and blown about by every wind of new teaching. We will not be influenced when people try to trick us with lies so clever, they sound like the truth … growing in every way more and more like Christ."

Assembling is vital to our ongoing spiritual health; it is also key to treating those wounds we incur along the way. Making a regular habit of getting together is like monitoring your diet, exercising, and getting regular blood work, checkups, and physicals. Doing so helps keep you spiritually healthy, developing a robust spiritual immunity to harmful mindsets that lead to unhealthy or sinful behaviors, and guarding against false teachings that may lead to spiritual weakening and death if not corrected.

Where I work, our physicians and surgeons may recommend various ancillary or secondary care services such as physical or occupational therapy in treating many orthopedic injuries. They may also suggest lifestyle changes like quitting smoking or losing weight. In the spiritual sense, our congregation's subsequent level of care is strongly encouraged to prevent and treat wounds through two different "ancillary care" or additional opportunities in the form of small groups and Delta groups (see below for explanation).

Developing deeper relationships with others is more challenging (but not impossible), especially in larger congregations. The typical exchange at church is, "Hey, how are you doing?" (Note: we do not expect them to answer that question!) The typical response is, "I am blessed!", "Great!", "Awesome, God is good!" Never mind the argument with your spouse as you pulled into the church parking lot. Sadly, many members are not comfortable "going forward" at the end of the sermon to share their struggle with the entire church family. If this isn't true where you worship, praise the Lord! That is a great blessing. Another echelon of care is often required to get past this spiritual dilemma.

Small groups are the *second* component of "making disciples" (they are nothing new but can be highly effective!). These assemblages are typically geographically located but not always a "small group" of the congregation that gets together regularly, maybe fifteen to twenty people tops. Our groups meet every other week; in some churches I have attended, they only met once a month or, at others, weekly. Small groups provide a perfect opportunity to "do life" together. As members of one another, we become each other's spiritual medics, caring for one another. Only in spending time together, getting to know one another more deeply, and being more fully known are where real bonds develop. Here, people often feel more secure in letting their guard down and allowing others in. More acute spiritual wounds are addressed and mended through fellowship, encouragement, and ongoing prayer. I cannot count the relationships and depth that wouldn't have developed were it not for small groups. Likewise, I cannot express the encouragement, growth, and healing that has occurred through sharing life with those brothers and sisters!

Taking that to the next echelon of spiritual care in "making disciples" is what we call "D (Delta) groups" or *discipleship groups*. These also are not new ideas but are very effective and something we have developed over several years under the leadership of our associate minister. We borrowed the practice from a congregation in Tennessee where one of our elder's sons attends, which is highly successful there. As one of my church mentors in Colorado, Ray Wallace, told me, "Only steal the good stuff!" These Delta groups consist of three to five Christian brothers or sisters who commit to meet weekly to share life's ups and downs, study, pray and spur one another on to higher spiritual growth. I cannot recommend them enough! They are life-changing if you are willing to commit and allow them to be a part of your spiritual life. If your "walk in the light" has become a limping meander, then a Delta group can be the spiritual ambulatory aid you need to be strengthened and get back in step with the Spirit—and that's okay! Remember the beginning of the chapter? There are no

Rambos in God's Army (that's not to say that you cannot become a highly trained spiritual commando doing real damage to the enemy).

Nevertheless, even the best efforts are not foolproof. When more severe spiritual injuries occur, the need for specific interventions is warranted. In orthopedic medicine (and trauma especially), some wounds require immediate surgery to restore things to their proper position and return to everyday life as quickly as possible (i.e., severe soft tissue trauma and fractured bones). With other types of trauma, surgery may be necessary only after all other conservative treatment measures have been exhausted and the pain is too great to deal with daily. Think of arthritis in your knees or hips. If you can't imagine that yet, enjoy it while it lasts!

Spiritually speaking, *ministers and elders* provide this next echelon of care in the local congregation. In general, based on life experience, knowledge of the Scriptures, and qualifications, these individuals can often provide care and counsel over time to help heal deeper wounds. Like many real seasoned combat medics, their field treatment abilities far exceed that of a lesser experienced warrior. In other instances, such as Special Forces, these individuals are highly-trained to administer a degree of care beyond basic first aid or even the EMT or paramedic (both first responders)—more like a physician assistant or nurse practitioner. Many ministers and elders have higher-level training or degrees and life experience, which frequently translates to a degree in counseling that enables them to provide the highest echelon or level of spiritual care. In instances where this is not the case, like our congregation, the staff, like all wise healthcare providers, know their scope of responsibility, what they are prepared to handle, and their limitations. In these instances, we have a list of local Christian counseling services. These are trained professionals whose treatment approaches are based on the Bible and God, who created you in His image. And as such, what you present with physically and mentally, is integrally tied to your spirituality (cf. Romans 12:1-2).

In closing, the one common thread through every echelon of care is the higher healing power of God and His word! I will leave you with the following passages that summarize this chapter very well.

- "I am the vine, you are the branches; the one who remains in Me, and I in him bears much fruit, for apart from Me you can do nothing" (John 15:5).

- "These things I have spoken to you so that in Me you may have peace. In the world you have tribulation but take courage; I have overcome the world" (John 16:33).

- "Now to Him who is able to do far more abundantly beyond all that we ask or think, according to the power that works within us" (Ephesians 3:20).

We certainly do and will incur physical wounds during our lifetime. And depending on their severity and duration, these can strain our spiritual lives and may cause us to question God. Ultimately, the wounds Christians suffer in this battle are spiritual, requiring a divine approach to healing. Only by remaining in Jesus can we access the power that overcomes the world!

PAUL FLORIO, U.S. Army, Veteran
MOS: Combat Medical Corpsman / Orthopedic Specialist
EMAIL: pflorio@fixbones.com

ENDNOTES:

1 *Combat Medic Specialist.* https://www.goarmy.com/careers-and-jobs/career-match/science-medicine/intensive-care/68w-combat-medic-specialist.html

2 Mark Batterson, *All In: You Are One Decision Away From a Totally Different Life.* (Grand Rapids: Zondervan, 2013), np.

CHAPTER 7
Spiritual Battle Scars

All Scriptures used are from the New International Version.

United States Navy SEALs are some of the most admired and elite military "special operators" worldwide, yet they too are subject to battle scars. Admiral William H. McRaven (U.S. Navy, Retired) served as commander of many SEAL teams. He authored *The Hero Code: Lessons Learned from Lives Well Lived*, citing examples of the men and women he worked with, pointing out characteristics or virtues of some of those colleagues and how they overcame countless adversities to develop admirable qualities.[1] In this chapter, I will address many hardships the Admiral records that may cause battle scars or disfigurements.

Battle scars might run more profound than we think. Often, injuries suffered on the battlefield can leave one with long-lasting physical scars or impairment, as well as emotional trauma that may last for decades or even a lifetime. Although initially trained as a combat medical corpsman or medic, I also received advanced Orthopedic Specialist training. Therefore, I have never witnessed firsthand the immediate effects of combat casualties. However, I was stationed at an Army Medical Center (CONUS Level V) designated to receive soldiers evacuated from the war zone to the U.S. for specialty care and more comprehensive recovery. [2] While stationed there, I witnessed many soldiers enduring emotional and physical effects of trauma.

During my military career, I not only earned the Expert Field Medical Badge, but I also assisted in training scores of soldiers to achieve the same coveted credential. This instruction entailed creating traumatic battle injuries and simulating that with moulage (i.e., synthetic tissue, bone, and blood) to represent an injury as accurately as possible. Trainees would then assess the wound(s) at a glance, take appropriate action and render first aid and other life-saving measures within a minimal time. During this training, it was easy to stop the scenario, provide necessary guidance and allow the soldier to continue the treatment they had begun. During testing, no advice could be given or received, and often the timed event was more stringent than would be absolutely necessary to treat the wound scenario. Although instructors staged multiple set-ups during training and testing, the stress of having numerous combat casualties, plus the thought of exposing yourself to live fire, noise, and so forth, is easy to imagine how difficult and stressful the job could become.

Christian soldiers can fall victim to the devil's schemes, resulting in emotional and spiritual wounds, which is why God admonishes us to "put on the full armor of God, so that you can take your stand against the devil's schemes" (Ephesians 6:11). In considering a Christian's daily life, a wound might occur through various sources: a simple "skinned knee" might appear as an individual stumbles in sin such as telling a *lie, speeding, etc.* Ensuring this does not become a battle scar depends on the self-care one delivers and/or aid the individual seeks from a Christian battle buddy. We are to "carry each other's burdens, and in this way you will fulfill the law of Christ" (Galatians 6:2). "Remember this: Whoever turns a sinner from the error of his way will save them from death and cover over a multitude of sins" (James 5:20).

How the soldier deals with the infraction determines the time it takes for healing. Using one of the previously mentioned examples, facing up to a *lie*, and expressing remorse to God and those affected by the untruth can often turn that "skinned knee" into healthy tissue again where the Holy Spirit, our conscience, and integrity help us not to tell further lies. "Therefore confess your sins to each other and pray for each other so that you may be healed. The prayer of a righteous person is powerful and effective" (James 5:16). In addition, you should "cast all your anxiety on him because he cares for you" (1 Peter 5:7). On the other hand, failing to repent can often lead to more lies and entanglement deepening the wound, creating a battle scar that can have serious, long-lasting consequences.

With the second example, simply taking your foot off the accelerator and doing your best to stay within the posted speed limit will have a similar positive effect on your psyche and soul. One might take exception with me regarding this matter, thinking that God does not address this particular issue as a sin, but I call your attention to this passage that says, "all wrongdoing is sin" (1 John 5:17).

During combat, medics put their life on the line for all injured warriors, whether fellow soldiers or civilians. Sometimes corpsmen must also treat enemy casualties within sight and sound. Christian soldiers are no different. We should prepare to render the soul-saving message at a moment's notice to our fellow Christian or non-believer to treat an immediate wound and help prevent the lasting battle scars that can accompany a wounded comrade. "Always be prepared to give an answer to everyone who asks you to give the reason for the hope that you have. But do this with gentleness and respect" (1 Peter 3:15). We hope and pray that each wounded warrior's faith will begin a healing process, yet sometimes that becomes tenuous or vague. "Blessed is the one who perseveres under trial because, having stood the test, that person will receive the crown of life that the Lord has promised to those who love him" (James 1:12). I say tenuous because, in the very next chapter, James states, "You see that a person is considered righteous by what they do and not by faith alone" (2:24). Subsequently, there is some action that must accompany one's faith.

One of the most grotesque wounds to simulate was a *severe burn*. I have seen a variety of them in my lifetime, but those burns over a large portion of the body can produce some of the most painful and life-threatening experiences. A spiritual burn on life's battlefield might be incurred simply because of your Christian faith and conviction and not as a direct result of one's failure or misstep. Undoubtedly, this is a dire situation that might create a lasting battle scar and possibly cause one to fall away from Christ to a point where spiritual death can occur. By their choosing, many evil people are devious and conniving. They will undermine your good intentions no matter how well you emulate Jesus or because you do your best to represent Him. How can we combat this scenario? "Dear friends, do not be surprised at the fiery ordeal that has come on you to test you, as though something strange were happening to you. But rejoice inasmuch as you participate in the sufferings of Christ, so that you may be overjoyed when his glory is revealed" (1 Peter 4:12-13).

Staying connected with a group of Christians who share your convictions is a great start. One cannot always surround himself with those of like faith, especially in the military; however, we can be vigilant to do so as often as possible. The book of James is another "go-to" place to help us cope with many trials that befall us. It certainly helps to instill God's word into our minds to give us strength and hope, knowing that He is always there and we can rely on His promises. Additionally, other parts of James' letter can help us understand actions that are acceptable to God and those that are not appropriate.

Traumatic limb amputations were always somewhat challenging to simulate during our training sessions. And yet, this is one of the most severe wounds that a combat medic must prepare to treat. The loss of a limb is highly traumatic. Having worked around these types of patients, I can speak with some authority; however, my most memorable experience is not from a battle wound but from a very close relative. This family member honorably served in the Navy as a gunner and crew chief on helicopters without incident, only to lose his lower right leg due to a rare kidney disease that caused arterial blood clots. While ministering to him shortly after the amputation, an emptiness in his heart was apparent. And yet, over the years, he has adapted very well, learning to drive with special controls, walking miles per day in his job, playing golf better than he ever had before, and generally, almost as if the situation had never occurred. His attitude toward losing his leg was the key to his recovery. I believe that he approached his situation daily with an optimism that his life would never be the same but possibly even better than ever.

The *death of a battle buddy* can also incur a devastating loss. These incidences can leave one with lasting scars if not approached with the right attitude. Looking beyond oneself is the key to recovery under these tragic circumstances. I began this chapter with a teaser regarding *The Hero Code*. As I recall, every hero mentioned displayed the biblical attitude or characteristic needed to overcome adversities many people cannot overcome. The apostle Paul provides a glimpse of this as he described Christ's perspective or attitude of being a servant and His obedience to the Father, as seen in Paul's letter to the church at Philippi (Philippians 2: 1-8).

In my continuing scenarios, this example can be classified as a *sucking chest wound*, a very severe injury that is life-threatening but does not cause immediate death. As inferred earlier, the devil is often the cause of Christian's battle wounds and scars. It may not be easy to imagine, but I am confident something similar has occurred in the life of a Christian. After many years of seemingly blissful marriage, one spouse decides they are no longer "in love" with the other. They may seek marital counseling, but one spouse entirely rejects it. Ultimately, divorce is a result. How devastating! So, how can this battle scar be healed? Only through time, Christian counseling, continuous Bible study, regular contact with Christian battle buddies, and countless hours of prayer. "But you, dear friends, build yourselves up in your most holy faith and pray in the Holy Spirit. Keep yourselves in God's love as you wait for the mercy of our Lord Jesus Christ to bring you to eternal life" (Jude 20-21).

Traumatic brain injuries (TBI) are head wounds that cannot be readily seen but often lead to permanent battle scars if not cared for accurately. However, sometimes these do not even manifest themselves until much later. In addition, more often than naught, they are incurred along with other battle injuries, so the trauma may not only be within the skull but accompanied by many external injuries making it more challenging to treat. Recognizing these wounds is the key to ensuring they do not become long-lasting battle scars. Like many injuries that can cause battle scarring, a TBI often leads to post-traumatic stress (PTS): a partial or complete mental and/or physical incapacity. These wounds require higher echelons of care, including long-term counseling and specialized medical treatment. In this example, the one who is the victim of such injuries often not only affects their recovery, but the victim's family may also fall prey to the devil's work in their lives. Christians need to surround this individual and family with great love, concern, and prayer regularly within this scenario.

We must practice forgiveness to prevent *open wounds* from becoming lasting battle scars. For instance, as mandated in the Bible, we must forgive others for the wrongs perpetrated against us. Jesus specifically taught forgiveness even in prayer: "And when you stand praying, if you hold anything against anyone, forgive them, so that your Father in heaven may forgive you your sins" (Mark 11:25). Many of us find it easier to forgive others while we cannot seem to forgive ourselves. Of course, I am not referring to forgiving our own sins, which is not humanly possible; only God has the power and authority to forgive sin. But the point is, we must not only pardon the injustices against us but also remove the guilt we feel due to our offenses. In listening to sermons for over fifty years, some preachers have professed that we could not forgive ourselves. I believe their premise is this: since we are not God, forgiveness is not ours to impart; yet if Jesus teaches forgiveness of others, it is only logical that we must pardon ourselves. I am not saying we need to forget our transgressions; however, it is wise to ignore them, so they do not open up *old wounds*. We need to learn from our mistakes and tap into our most incredible resource, God Himself, to help us prevent those misdeeds in the future.

In closing, while we live *in* this world, we are not *of* this world. Jesus stressed this principle in talking with His skeptics and disciples. As Christians in the Lord's Army, we can avoid many, if not all, battle scars if we will only realize this truth and live like we truly believe in this principle. The only battle scars in heaven will be those of Jesus—ours will have vanished—HALLELUJAH! (cf. John 20:27) [EDITOR'S NOTE: check out the song "Scars in Heaven" by Casting Crowns for its message.]

MELVYN CARAWAY, U.S. Army, Retired
MOS: Chief Medical NCO/Combat Medical/Orthopedic Specialist
EMAIL: mgcaraway@comcast.net

ENDNOTE:

1 Admiral McRaven, William H. *The Hero Code: Lessons Learned From Lives Well Lived.* (New York: Grand Central Publishing, 2021), 3-177.

2 *Level V*. https://jts.amedd.army.mil/assets/docs/assessments/Afghan-Trauma-System-Review-18-Mar-2010.pdf2

CHAPTER 8

Spiritual Medicine and Treatment Plan

All Scripture references are from the New King James Version unless indicated otherwise.

I once heard a saying that went something like this: "If you are casual about the way you live your spiritual life, you will become a spiritual casualty of Satan." When the truth of this thought sinks in, you should be immediately motivated to perform a spiritual inventory of how you are currently living life.

We may find it easier to pass judgments about others throughout our day instead of examining ourselves. However, when it comes time to take our spiritual inventory, it is easy to become blinded by pride or be in a state of denial of our negative thought processes. Just because we can speak the correct church jargon, attend worship service, read our Bibles, and sing church hymns doesn't mean we are spiritually aligned with Jesus. He says this in Matthew 7:21-23,

> Not everyone who says to Me, 'Lord, Lord,' shall enter the kingdom of heaven, but he who does the will of My Father in heaven. Many will say to Me in that day, 'Lord, Lord, have we not prophesied in Your name, cast out demons in Your name, and done many

wonders in Your name?' And then I will declare to them, 'I never knew you; depart from Me, you who practice lawlessness!'

Therefore, ingesting our daily spiritual medicine as prescribed from the Word of God is imperative. You see, from the very beginning, everything hung on the Word of God (i.e., our cure): "In the beginning was the Word, and the Word was with God, and the Word was God" (John 1:1). Therefore, the Bible contains the spiritual medicine and proper treatment needed to cure us of our disease of sin.

WHAT ARE THE GOALS OF MODERN MEDICINE AND THEIR TREATMENTS?

According to the National Library of Medicine,

The goals of medicine encompass the relief of pain and suffering, the promotion of health and the prevention of disease, the forestalling of death and the promoting of a peaceful death, and the cure of disease when possible and the care of those who can not be cured." [1]

While we can see the benefits of our modern-day medicines and treatments, we do not want to neglect the medication and therapy for our souls. "For what will it profit a man if he gains the whole world, and loses his own soul?" (Mark 8:36).

No matter who you are, where you reside or work, you live in a spiritual warzone. There are only two sides to this conflict and only two Commanders-in-Chief. You are either fighting on the side of God or Satan—there is no in-between. One side will give you the ultimate victory in Jesus, while the other will send you to eternal damnation with Satan (Revelation 21:7-8).

Which side have you chosen today, and are you one hundred percent sure? You will experience emotional, physical, and spiritual pain as you continue to fight through this war. The temptation Satan wields and uses against us is the source of this pain and anguish. There are no lows he will not sink to trap us in sin. As part of our spiritual treatment plan, we must avoid certain things. The Bible says,

> Do not love the world or the things in the world. If anyone loves the world, the love of the Father is not in him. For all that is in the world—the lust of the flesh, the lust of the eyes, and the pride of life—is not of the Father but is of the world. And the world is passing away, and the lust of it; but he who does the will of God abides forever. (1 John 2:15-17)

Look around and see the corruption of this world. Now, remember to take your spiritual inventory. Keep an eye out for how you may allow the spiritual hosts of wickedness to hinder your spiritual growth. Stay sharp and focused. In Ephesians 6:12, God's message is clear: when we focus our fight on another human being, we are fighting the wrong battle. "For we do not wrestle [struggle] not against flesh and blood, but against principalities, against powers, against the rulers of the darkness of this age, against spiritual hosts of wickedness in the heavenly places."

We must be careful, for Satan masquerades or transforms himself into an angel of light (2 Corinthians 11:14). He will often disguise evil as something good to deceive us! That is why it is essential always to stay close to God's will as revealed in His Word. Only then will we be able to discern or recognize what is of God versus what comes from the Evil One.

In Romans 3:23, Paul reminds us that "everyone has sinned; we all fall short of God's glorious standard" (NLT). If we say that we do not and have never sinned, we make Christ out to be a liar! (1 John 1:10) Ever since the fall of humanity in the Garden of Eden, every person who reached the age of account accountability has sinned. There is no escape from it. This sin separates us from God because He is holy, and evil can never stand in His presence. But all hope isn't lost because God has done something miraculous, something we can't do for ourselves.

There is only one remedy for sin: the precious blood of Jesus! The blood of Christ cleanses us from all unrighteousness, the very unrighteousness that causes us to sin and separates us from God in the first place. Jesus accomplished this by living the perfect human life, the kind that we could never live on our own. Then, He took the ultimate punishment for that sin—death on a cross. Jesus spent three days in the grave, then looked death in the face and denied its power over Him. Jesus rose from the grave and is alive forever! I love how He is described in John 1:29, "The next day John saw Jesus coming toward him, and said, 'Behold! The Lamb of God who takes away the sin of the world!'" The truth found here is both simple and profound. Jesus takes away our sins! And what is the result? We can once again have a deep and powerful relationship with God because sin no longer separates us. The power that sin once had over our lives is no more, and we can walk in the treatment plan of abundant freedom of Christ.

One of the most common pitfalls in the spiritual warzone we must avoid is playing the victim role. It is so easy to get wrapped up in our pain and disappointments. The best remedy for not playing the role of a victim is to remember what Jesus Christ did for you and all humanity. So, how can we find healing amid the wounds we sustain while in the spiritual warzone? It all starts with focusing our hearts on Jesus, our best Physician. He is the source of profound healing and restoration in our lives.

Luke 24:13-33 tells us a powerful story about recognizing Jesus' presence. Two of His believers walked along the road to the village of Emmaus after Jesus' resurrection, discussing the events that had recently occurred with His crucifixion. Then, the risen Christ Himself comes and walks beside them! But these two believers do not recognize Him. They speak as if He is just someone who has come up and walked alongside them. When Jesus asks what they are discussing, they talk about the recently transpired occurrences. They seemed downcast and discouraged over it, even though Jesus is right there with them! He then opens the Scriptures to them, explaining that these events are precisely what the Word of God foretold. This was the *spiritual medicine* they so desperately needed! This divine prescription brought them healing, comfort, and encouragement, though they did not recognize Jesus. It was only later that they realized just what had really happened on that road!

How often does this happen in our own lives? Jesus' presence is always with us, yet we often act like He is not there. We are constantly calling out to Him, looking for ways to enter His presence, and attempting to activate His power in our lives when Jesus is right there, eager to give us the spiritual treatment only He can provide.

Sometimes it is easier to recognize Jesus in the brighter moments of our lives. However, He is there in the darkest moments as well. That is when we must cling to Him most! Just as He did with those two believers, Jesus will open up the Scriptures (e.g., providing spiritual insight) to you as well, shedding light into the darkness of your life and bringing healing to your heart. You must follow the *spiritual treatment plan* prescribed in His Word. Our diagnosis? The cancer of sin manifest in our flesh, which lives within our hearts and minds. So, what do we need? A spiritual blood exchange or transfusion. A transfusion takes whole or parts of blood and infuses it into a patient's bloodstream through a vein. For the most part, the blood to be used is donated by another person (although one can "bank" their blood for future use in surgery). Just as a blood transfusion can save someone with a life-threatening injury or disease, the blood of Christ saves us from the spiritual death and separation from God that results from our sin and brings us salvation that leads to eternal life! And it is all possible through what He did on the cross through the spilling of His blood.

> Don't you know that all of us who were baptized into Christ Jesus were baptized into his death? We were therefore buried with him through baptism into death in order that, just as Christ was raised from the dead through the glory of the Father, we too may live a new life. For if we have been united together in the likeness of His death, certainly we also shall be *in the likeness of His* resurrection. (Romans 6:3-5)

While this is our ultimate source of healing and renewal, we must also take our *daily spiritual prescriptions*. We must infuse our lives with love, joy, truth, and peace at the start of every day; otherwise, the cancer of sin will destroy our hearts and lives. Spiritual medicine is the antidote to sin! We must continually combat the corruption that can plague our hearts with God's treatment plan.

We will now look at three different types of doctors who treat physical maladies in this life and then compare them to the spiritual healing we receive through Christ. First is a *cardiologist* or heart doctor. These professionals specialize in treating heart conditions and diseases and helping patients manage their disorders as much as possible. This specialist can diagnose and treat any symptoms, heart conditions, and potential illnesses with various remedies, including medications, surgery, etc. Jesus, the ultimate Heart Specialist, can treat our spiritual heart condition in even more profound ways. In Matthew 6:21, He says, "for where your treasure is, there your heart will be also." What does He mean by this? It is where we place our time, effort, and energies that will determine the course of our life. When we commit ourselves to worldly things, we will live sin-sick lives. However, when we choose to live for Christ, our hearts will bear the excellent fruit (vitamins) of the spirit of His Spirit found in Galatians 5:22-23.

Secondly, a *neurologist* is a physician having expertise in neurology and trained to diagnose and treat disorders of the brain, nerves, and spinal cord. Jesus likewise can heal our minds and prepare us mentally for spiritual warfare. Colossians 3:1-2 says, "If [since] then you were raised with Christ, seek those things which are above, where Christ is, sitting at the right hand of God. Set your mind on things above, not on things on the earth." This verse reminds us that what we think about is important because it will determine how we live our lives. When we saturate our minds with God's Word and truth, godly living will result from it. That is because this lifestyle shapes our mindset, our mindset shapes our actions, and our actions dictate who we are and Whose we are.

And lastly, an *optometrist* is another healthcare professional who provides primary vision care ranging from sight testing and correction to diagnosing, treating, and managing vision changes. Jesus, our spiritual Eye Specialist, stated that "if the eye is unhealthy then the whole body is unhealthy" (Matthew 6:23). Therefore, our heart, body, mind, and soul must be focused on Christ and not on the things of the world! Through the spiritual disciplines of daily Bible reading, prayer, and fellowship, we have the blessed opportunity to draw closer and closer to God in every way. When we do, He will equip us with everything we need to succeed on the spiritual battlefield and defeat Satan's influences in our lives. "His divine power has given to us all things that pertain to life and godliness, through the knowledge of Him who called us by glory and virtue" (2 Peter 1:3).

Part of this is making sure that we keep perspective. While we live in a sin-fallen world, and things here may not always turn out as we hope they would, God's plans will prevail. We can still trust in His promise of eternity; He will never let us down, leave us, or forsake us. We must always keep our eyes on God's kingdom first, not the things of this world (Matthew 6:33).

2 Corinthians 4:16-18 reads,

Therefore we do not lose heart. Even though our outward man is perishing, yet the inward *man* is being renewed day by day. For our light affliction, which is but for a moment, is working for us a far more exceeding *and* eternal weight of glory, while we do not look at the things which are seen, but at the things which are not seen. For the things which are seen *are* temporary, but the things which are not seen *are* eternal.

We must never forget that the pain of this life is temporary, while the reward we receive in Christ is eternal. While the world we live in now is unpredictable, tumultuous, and full of many trials, we will spend eternity in a plan of perfect peace, harmony, and love. The work we do here for the Lord reaps eternal consequences in the life to come!

It is essential to live for Jesus and share Him with others. God desires that as many as possible come to the knowledge of His Son and place their faith in Him so they can enter eternity. As God's children, we have the responsibility to continue the redemptive work of Christ and spread His love to every corner of the earth, as told to us in the Great Commission found in Matthew 28:16-20.

In closing, God has placed each of His people in the church as it pleases Him, according to His purpose (cf. Acts 2:47; 1 Corinthians 12:18). God has given us the remarkable honor and responsibility of spreading His Kingdom here on earth until the day that Jesus returns and ushers us into the fullness of all eternity. That is why we must live fully for Christ. There is no room to be lukewarm here. We must give everything we have to live our godly lives according to Jesus's example. Our hearts must echo the words we find in Jeremiah 20:9: "But if I say, 'I will not mention his word or speak anymore in his name,' his word is in my heart like a fire, a fire shut up in my bones. I am weary of holding it in; indeed, I cannot" (NIV). When we do this, we will fight, live on God's side, and have a place with Him for eternity.

HARRY WASHINGTON III, U.S. Air Force, Retired
AFSC: Administrative Specialist
EMAIL: drharry4@gmail.com

EDITOR'S NOTE: Harry is a Licensed Clinical Christian Counselor with a Ph.D. in Clinical Christian Counseling and is now a Christian Motivational Speaker and a Christian YouTuber. His channels are *God's Virtual School* and *God's Greater Love*.

ENDNOTE:

1 D. Callahan, *Managed care and the goals of medicine*. J Am Geriatric Soc. 1998 Mar;46(3):385-8. https://pubmed.ncbi.nlm.gov/9514393/

CHAPTER 9
Spiritual Recovery

All Scriptures are from the New International Version.

I first entered the U.S. Army in 1977 as an enlisted soldier. Basic training was tough. The drill sergeant would "smoke us" to muscle failure, then bark out, "Recover!" That meant we had to get on our feet as quickly as possible and stand in the position of attention. Standing there as if nothing had happened.

Sometimes life "smokes us." Add to that, our nation asks a lot from us. Family separations. Deployments. Stress. Injuries. Trauma. Of course, we accept these hardships as loyal Soldiers, Airmen, Sailors, Coast Guardsmen, Marines, and now, Guardians (Space Force). It is part of the job description. Plus, we are loyal—to the mission, our Nation, and our battle buddies. Then, we redeploy home or become civilians and bark the order, "Recover!" We start trying to live the way ahead as if nothing serious happened. Acting as if nothing terrible or stressful happened is not altogether awful. We are tough guys and gals, or we would never have gone into the military. We learned to "suck it up and drive on." That's good.

We need to be strong—God's Army Strong! We must be careful not to make things appear worse than they are. We must persevere. And yet, we are still human. We all have a breaking point. We need to know when that point is approaching. Stress is not your friend if there is too much. That stress might be from reliving bad events, guilt, or having too much on your plate. Then, stress is the gift that keeps on giving. Some people become anxious. Others become depressed. We will get to where we need help when these things add up. Get the support when you need it. Throw away stigmas. I go to a psychiatrist provided by the VA. So what? It doesn't hurt. Sometimes I feel like it doesn't help a lot either. But who knows? Getting that kind of help may be doing more good than I realize.

It is essential to have people around you who care about you. However, pick your friends carefully. It might not be so good for your recovery if they are helping you drown your sorrows at the bar. Even if you decide on your friends from church, you must choose them carefully. Many well-meaning churchgoers will spiritualize things that may mean very little to you. Others may try to give some check-the-box remedy by trying to get you to be more religious. Be careful! Some people make religion harder than God does! Look for those who have your best interest in view, have empathy, and are available.

Now, in the rest of this chapter, let us turn toward how you think spiritually and what you can do to recover. Let us also look at how spiritual focus can move you forward to a better place—no matter how healthy or sick you are. You can do many things to relieve stress and grow as a person.

I AM REALLY BUSY

Is *'Being Busy' the New Status Symbol?* This is the title of an article by Dr. Rick Nauert, a doctorate associate professor for Rocky Mountain University of Health Professionals.[1] His article hit many news outlets a few years ago, including national-level news syndicates. Listen in the hallway: "Hey Jill, how are things going?" "Oh, I'm okay—just really busy." Probably we all are—especially among overachievers like us. I remember the first time I realized that I am a driven person. During a break between semesters at college, I was sitting outside by myself as the weather was perfect. Still, I felt like I needed to be doing something. I was fidgety and a little anxious. I could not place why I was feeling like that. Then it dawned on me: I was not able to relax.

Dr. Nauert explains that people used to associate success with possessing a lot of toys, having a big house, and having plenty of leisure time to enjoy. "Americans increasingly perceive busy and overworked people as having high status."[2] Why? High-status Americans a generation ago might have boasted about their lives of leisure. Still, today they're more likely to engage in humblebrag, telling those around them how they "have no life" or "desperately need a vacation." Here is the psychological part: "People's social-mobility beliefs are psychologically driven by the perception that busy individuals possess desirable characteristics, leading them to be viewed as scarce and in demand." Maybe put another way, "I work hard because they need me. And, I need to be needed." [3] If I am busy, it makes me look important.

I heard long ago, "What do you do if you have too many irons in the fire? You make the fire bigger." What are some of the irons in your fire? They are not just work-related. We add irons with our kids and grandkids. We add irons by other commitments. We add irons even within our church. We keep piling on irons. Busy is good. We need to be productive. Hard work pays off. We want to feel like we contribute, and we need to contribute. Busy is bad. We accumulate stress—and it can be self-inflicted. Things pull us in a hundred different directions, so focusing on the main effort becomes difficult. This non-stop stress can be bad for your health. This hectic lifestyle can take a toll on your family—the quality time is not there.

THE SABBATH PRINCIPLE

So, let me tell you about the Sabbath principle. The Bible tells us that God created all things in six days; then, on the seventh day, he rested. What does that mean? He did not need a break. He was still holding his creation together. So, why did God "rest?" The cultural background for the Genesis message is set in ancient Sumer (one of the oldest civilizations in ancient Mesopotamia). The Sumerians believed in many gods; their goddess Tiamat was the mother of Chao, and the other gods conquered her. From what was left over, they made the earth and people. Here is the interesting part: the Sumerians had a Sabbath too. However, it was much different from the Genesis Sabbath. The Sumerians were afraid Tiamat would come back. The Sumerians lived in fear and made sacrifices on their Sabbath to keep Tiamat from coming back and collapsing creation into chaos again. In contrast, in Genesis, God rested on the Sabbath (2:2). There was no fear that the world would fall apart (this verse shows a picture of chaos brought to order).

Your world will not fall apart because you take a knee from the rat race. Have you ever heard the phrase, "take a knee"? In the Army, soldiers work hard. Some jobs require long marches. They must walk miles through rough terrain with a lot of weight on their back. Along the way, their leaders will say, "Seek shade, take a knee, and drink water." We need to take a knee. Your world will not turn to chaos if you do. Instead, this will actually allow you to be more productive. In the Law of Moses, there is even a Sabbath for the farmland. Israel was told not to cultivate and plant every seventh year (Exodus 23:11; Leviticus 25:4). Now we know about crop rotations. Letting the land rest allows the soil to recover its nutrients. The Sabbath was a big deal in Israel's history and during Jesus' time. As I understand Him, Jesus did not give the Sabbath to *not* work on a certain day; He made it for His people (Mark 2:27).

You can take the day off and still miss the Sabbath principle. How many take their work home? How many check their work e-mails on your day off? Or worse, on your vacation? The Sabbath is a time to rejuvenate. Whether it is Saturday, Sunday, or a weeknight, take the time to hit the reset button and focus on your Maker and your family. Dr. Laurence Susser once said, "Workaholics commit slow suicide by refusing to allow the child inside them to play." [4] What do you do for fun? Do you take the time for it? Can you do it without thinking about your responsibilities? What do you do for fun with your spouse, kids, and grandkids? A friend of mine, Chaplain Paul Ramsey, told me of a poster: "Too busy not to pray."

What do you do to focus on your Maker? Sometimes I relax (I mean collapse). I am convinced that sometimes, God forces me to slow down when I get sick. I still have a hard time trying to relax. I feel like I need to be doing something. I am getting better, though. It takes a conscious decision to let things go—at least for a little while. Again, I encourage you to "take a knee," and hit the reset button. Do not take life too seriously—you will never make it out alive. Use the Sabbath principle: take time for your family and yourself and focus on your Creator. Make that choice, and life will go much better for you.

SPIRITUAL EXERCISE

So, now that you have been "taking a sabbath"— "taking a knee," it is time to get busy again. However, this is about getting busy constructively—by learning to bulk up with spiritual exercise. Godly spiritual empowerment begins with your relationship with Him. Let us explore suggestions for developing your devotional life despite a busy schedule.

BIBLICAL FOUNDATIONS

When considering biblical figures who were true to God, you will often find spiritual discipline. The Apostle Paul encouraged the young evangelist, Timothy, to "train yourself to be godly" (1 Timothy 4:7). Acceptable worship toward God comes from a place of thanksgiving and humility. Some met Him in ordinary times, others in distressing times. Scripture does not tell us how to approach God. Rather, the impression is that He approaches people, so you must be receptive for the moment for renewal to happen. Paul describes a war against the forces of darkness (Ephesians 6:12). The power of prayer (verse 18) becomes the focal point for the struggle. And even in moments when our faith waivers, Jesus said a mustard seed-sized faith can move mountains (Matthew 17:20-21). Christianity is about a triumphant life (Ephesians 3:20). Before Jesus' arrest in the Garden of Gethsemane, spiritual darkness was at its greatest hour. The powers of Satan thought they triumphed when they slew the Lamb of God. Rising from the grave, the King of kings rallied His people to fight the good fight. There are still dark hours today. However, Jesus the Victor is only a stone's throw away.

SPIRITUAL DISCIPLINE

Spiritual discipline means setting personal issues, day-to-day work, and recreation priorities. Practicing spiritual discipline helps you recharge your spiritual batteries. It keeps you focused on your Creator; it enables you to become a more balanced human being and allows you to counter self-destructive choices. The following spiritual disciplines serve to convict, affirm, heal, mature, and bring joy. I hope you give them a chance.

PRAYING

Prayer is hard work. I used to try to set aside time every morning for prayer. Not anymore. Maybe I have too much on my mind—about what I must do that day. I will pray while lying in bed, getting ready to sleep. Then, I fall asleep when I am praying. However, I am not too worried about when and how much I pray. More importantly, my mind almost always goes to God throughout the day. Paul said to "pray continually" (1 Thessalonians 5:17). In the verses before and after, he says, "rejoice always" and "give thanks in all circumstances." Prayer, just like joy and thankfulness, is a state of mind. When I hear someone arguing, I will say something to God about it. When I hear some good news—like someone getting out of the hospital—under my breath, I will say, "Thank you, Lord." Prayer is not a religious check-the-box ritual. Rather, prayer is something that comes out of your awareness of

God in this world. Still, probably the more you put into prayer, the more He will do through and with you. Terry Muck suggests three strategies for making prayer more prominent in your life. [5] *First*, he tells setting up a system of accountability. In other words, find someone with whom to join in prayer regularly or someone who will help keep the commitment to prayer.

Second, give yourself both positive and negative reinforcements. For example, someone might go without breakfast until they spend some time praying. Another uses stoplights to trigger a prayer. *Third*, connect prayer to a physical act. Some pray aloud while others use three-by-five cards to list prayer requests—they review them and pray over them while walking. Many pray while running, swimming, or during some other exercise. As Muck explains,

> The obvious goal of all these practices is to associate prayer with something beneficial to help overcome the lethargy that can strike us all ... Our body language can help us remember that we are talking to a living, active God who is present, powerful, and listening. [6]

MEDITATING

One time I went to a workshop related to counseling. The facilitator had us sit in a circle and start doing breathing exercises. Slowly and softly, she would say, "Breath in and hold your breath. Now, slowly breathe out." After getting relaxed, "Now empty your mind. Let your thoughts go. Release your thoughts into the universe." While some people may find this beneficial, I did not. I just got sleepy—maybe my sleep apnea was kicking in.

In the Bible, meditation is not an emptying of the mind. Instead, it reflects the will of God. Every Scripture mentioning meditation describes contemplation on God's law and the Lord's ways (e.g., Psalm 1:2 and 119:15). Meditation and silence describe the practice of stilling the soul. It is a way to be quiet so you can hear God. You might think about something that prompts you to pray. However, the goal is to listen. The Holy Spirit may prompt you by speaking to your conscience. He may use a memory or possibly an insight you gained. Trying to fill solitude with prayer is like talking to a friend without listening to her response. Meditative silence may lead to a conviction of sin and subsequent confession.

FASTING

I go without food for twelve hours before having my blood drawn at the lab. I do not like it, though, as I like to eat. The monks in Europe during Medieval times used to fast a lot. That is when they perfected beer (they called it liquid bread). I guess that might make fasting more fun. In the Old Testament, we see where people would fast because they were in crisis—like sorrow over some horrible thing they did or because of a terrible loss—like a child dying. Most of us probably do not feel like eating when in distress. In New Testament times, fasting became a religious practice. It became so much a part of the Jewish religion that many thought it was strange that Jesus and His disciples did not fast (Matthew 9:14; Mark 2:18; and Luke 5:33). In the Sermon on the Mount, when Jesus says, "When you fast," it implies the practice would continue to be a discipline for His followers to come (Matthew 6:16). However, He warns us not to let fasting be a means for lifting one's spirituality before others (Matthew 6:16-18). Some fast as a way to strengthen prayer or to seek God's guidance (Ezra 8:23).

Be careful not to use fasting so God will do something for you—like thinking He will be more likely to hear your prayers. Avoid this pitfall. Instead, it is better to understand fasting as a means of preparing the heart for openness to God's direction or to make ourselves more in tune with a prayerful attitude. Fasting can heighten your awareness of spiritual things. You may find that you resist cravings for more than just food. One warning, though—only fast if you are healthy enough to do it. Do not try it if you have trouble with blood sugar or other medical problems. Or, you may modify what you eat—like giving up something you like for a week. Regardless, it is about your determination to focus on God's presence.

HEARING SCRIPTURE

Scripture reading and study was a discipline only a few could enjoy during biblical history. Most people had access to the Scripture by hearing it read and expounded upon in the Temple or the synagogue (John 7:14-15; and Luke 4:16-17). Reflecting upon the Word of God was often passed along to family members through oral tradition. However, when portions of Scripture became more available, God's people hungered to read it. Read and study for devotional purposes. Researching Scripture for a lesson to share is also beneficial. However, the passage for the lesson may not be the one needed for what you are going through right now. When you read for devotional purposes, you gain spiritual momentum. I like to focus on passages that focus on praise and the majesty of God. Meditate upon, memorize, or rewrite the passage to internalize God's Word. Read devotional writings; discover classical devotional literature in addition to current writers.

PRACTICING LIFE

The Book of Proverbs is a collection of wisdom about practical devotion, including seeking a godly life. God challenges believers in such statements as: "you ought to live holy and godly lives" (2 Peter 3:11b) and "be perfect, therefore, as your heavenly Father is perfect" (Matthew 5:48). The Sermon on the Mount has been called the "Constitution of Christianity." Practical devotion also includes service—the fulfillment of the second great command to "love your neighbor as yourself" (Leviticus 19:18; Matthew 22:39; and Mark 12:31). When you know your life is tracking with God's lifestyle, there is empowerment in your soul. Of course, a healthy humility knows none of this is possible without the grace of Jesus (1 John 1:8-10). As one walks in the light, there is joy (1 John 1:4-7), from which comes another practice that elevates the soul—singing (James 5:13b). A lifestyle starts to build so that your life becomes a living sacrifice in worship to God (Romans 12:1). Use the spiritual gifts God gives you. Become more giving—with your time and money, which will help you become less selfish and more responsive to others. Serving others combats spiritual stagnation and fosters spiritual growth.

JOURNALING

Journaling puts your life down on paper and can answer questions like "Who am I?" "Why do I feel …?" "In what ways am I changing?" Honesty is key. The temptation is to cast yourself in a favorable light. You may choose to keep your journal private, or you may want to share it with someone you trust to engage in a dialogue about spiritual growth. This exercise serves its purpose fully if you are willing to explore your soul's depths and come to grips with it. As you record prayers answered and blessings gained, you can look back at what you wrote—maybe years later. The pages may pop into the present as a great source of encouragement. You will likely find you made a lot of progress with your goal setting.

ENJOYING YOURSELF

Personal retreats are awesome. You might go on a camping trip. Use your vacation to the mountains or the beach as a personal spiritual retreat. Choose a place that is private and free from distractions. Plan to be gone at least twenty-four hours. You may have a planned time for prayer, reading, reflection, walking, etc. You may choose to be more spontaneous. The important point is to use the time to be receptive to God's presence. Take time for recreation, which helps build relationships. Recreation is also a diversion from daily activities; however, it probably benefits everyone the most by providing an attitude adjustment. Balance is learned. Have fun. Be willing to laugh at yourself and not take yourself too seriously.

GETTING TO KNOW YOU BETTER

Try getting outside feedback. Some people use formal performance evaluations and psychological testing to get external feedback. Testing can reveal personality traits, leadership profiles, and mental and emotional functioning. Many may hesitate, fearing what they might find out. Still, this is a way to do it if you want to dig deep. Whatever you find out—talk to God about it. You can also get good feedback from professional counseling and accountability groups. These groups are also great for emotional support. Counseling may be helpful if one uncovers memories or feelings that seem unbearable or overwhelming. If you choose an accountability group, find three to five people you can trust and people who want to grow spiritually. Accountability groups also offer an atmosphere of transparency. Commit to encouraging each other and to confidentiality.

SINGING

Singing lifts the soul. This is not just a matter of listening to Christian music. You sing too—even if you are not that good at it. Whether singing with others, in a small group, with a CD in the car or just from memory, spiritual songs penetrate the soul with conviction and joy. Singing is related to prayer because the words often lift inner desires to the Almighty. When you cannot find the words for praise, singing can do the job because they seem too repetitious, from prayer to prayer. Rather than merely listening, lifting your voice to God helps you uniquely internalize the Word.

BUILDING RELATIONSHIPS

God never made us to be alone. He made us for each other. This is especially true for our brothers and sisters who follow Jesus. Going to worship service on Sunday morning should not be for what you can get out of it. There are two critical reasons for being together to worship with other believers. First, as you focus upon the majesty of God in an aura of reverence or celebration, there is a sense that God is near. Second, besides encouraging yourself, this atmosphere is edifying to all involved. There is mutual bonding. There is a feeling of unity, purpose, and spiritual power. Renewal comes from shared pain, joy, and experiences. If someone is experiencing a blessing or answered prayer, their joy is multiplied when shared with others. Renewal also comes when Christians share their lives in step with the spirit (1 Corinthians 14:26). One of the most spiritual things you can do is build relationships. A failing marriage will bring you down. A rebellious teenager is distressing. For some of us, the damage is already done. However, if you let your Christlike love shine on your family, you can prevent further injury or repair existing problems. It may take time. Relationships tend to weaken unless an effort is made to cultivate them. However, working on our relationships is the most important spiritual discipline you can practice. Remember the second greatest commandment principle: "Love your neighbor as yourself" (Matthew 19:19).

RECOVER!

Do I do all these exercises? No. I don't really see myself as a spiritual athlete. I don't always find time to practice the sabbath principle. That's okay. It was not easy when you were in the military and had to do those long road marches. Still, you kept going. That's what will help you as you grow spiritually. Many find difficulty in finding adequate time for spiritual disciplines. It would be great to spend an hour or more in prayer every day or spend a day every week in solitude. Time restraints then contribute to feelings of guilt, frustration, or superficiality in faith. Richard Foster says, "Superficiality is the curse of our age. The doctrine of instant satisfaction is a primary spiritual problem. The desperate need today is not for a greater number of intelligent or gifted people, but for deep people." [7] Practicing any spiritual discipline does not need to be measured by time. Brief moments of silence, prayer, and service throughout the day will significantly benefit more than not making an effort. An act of service can be as simple as sending an encouraging e-mail to someone. Utter a ten-second thanksgiving prayer when hearing good news about a co-worker.

As we close, take a five-minute moment of silence sometime during the day, having the receptionist hold your calls for ten minutes. Preaching and gospel music can be heard over the car's stereo system during commuting to and from work. The idea is to allow the practice of spiritual disciplines despite a busy schedule. The more time you spend, the better. "Recover!" However, don't ignore yourself when you need help. Better yet, practice the suggestions in this chapter. You will become stronger. You will become more balanced. You will find healing for your soul. You will be a spiritual warrior who will give others courage. God bless you for being on point in God's mission.

GARY PAYNE, D. Min., U.S. Army, Retired
MOS: Chaplain
EMAIL: gary.g.payne@gmail.com

EDITOR NOTE: Gary is Chairman of the Chaplaincy Endorsement Committee for his church on behalf of all federal chaplains under him.

ENDNOTES:

1 Rick Nauert, "*Is 'Being Busy' the New Status Symbol?*" https://psychcentral.com, March 27, 2017 [EDITOR'S NOTE: this article is no longer on the website. July 23, 2022]

2 "*Is 'Being Busy' the New Status Symbol?*"

3 "*Is 'Being Busy' the New Status Symbol?*"

4 Dr. Lawrence Susser, "*Careers: Watching Workaholics at Play.*" https://www.washingtonpost.com/archive/lifestyle/1981/07/07/careers-watching-workaholics-at-play/e0866073-09ef-48cd-a591-a41a23c1fd0b/

5 Terry C. Muck, "*Personal Prayer.*" *Leadership Handbook of Management and*

Administration. ed. James D. Berkley. (Grand Rapids: Baker Book House, 1994), 30.

6 Muck, "*Personal Prayer.*" 31.

7 Richard J. Foster, *Celebration of Discipline: The Path to Spiritual Growth*. rev. ed. (San Francisco: Harper, 1988), 1.

CHAPTER 10
Spiritual Victory: V-J Day

All Scriptures are from the New American Standard Bible.

Comparative to all military matters throughout time on earth and in heaven, *earthly* military forces are *physical* and thus *temporal,* while the *heavenly* military forces are *spiritual* and *eternal.* For example, the United States has historically, militarily, and officially recognized September 2, 1945, as the day Japan formally surrendered to the Allies bringing World War II to an end. Since then, that day has been referred to as V-J or Victory-Over-Japan Day. However, in the physical and temporal realm, this moniker will end if or when the U.S. (at least as we know it) ceases to exist. The Bible teaches us that God raises nations when they suit His purpose and then brings them down when they willfully go beyond His goal (Job 12:23; Habakkuk 1:6, 11-13; 3:16; Acts 17:26).

Conversely, in heaven's spiritual and eternal domain, the Scriptures infer there is a V-J or *Victory-In-Jesus* Day for all believing and obedient Christian warriors who die faithful to Him. For instance, Jesus sent a Holy Spirit-inspired, biblically recorded written message via the apostle John to His battling warriors in the church at Smyrna (e.g., Asia Minor, modern Turkey) in the middle A.D. 90s.

While engaged in a daily life-and-death struggle against satanic Imperial Roman persecution, Christ's message of encouragement to them stated in part, "Be faithful until [physical] death, and I will give you the crown of [eternal] life" (Revelation 2:10, NASB Update). One commentator on Revelation wrote of this verse, "'Be thou faithful unto death' literally means 'Have unto-death faithfulness.'" [1] As spiritual warriors, we must engage our arch-enemies of Satan, sin, and death every day we live, 24/7/365.

Accordingly, whenever faithful spiritual combatants on this earthly battlefield die physically, they receive and will forever enjoy their triumph in the spiritual and eternal realm. There are two significant differences between the U.S.' literal V-J (and V-E) Day and God's heavenly and figurative victory day. *Firstly*, America's conquest of Japan has come and gone. Besides the WWII nuclear blast ruins in Hiroshima and Nagasaki, most of what remains are the memories of the physically and/or spiritually wounded warriors who lived through it and are still alive today. *Secondly*, those who have triumphed through Jesus will live forever with all faithfully spiritually wounded warriors (or citizens) in the kingdom who have passed from this life into eternity (Philippians 3:20-21). Accordingly, it has existed before creation and will perpetuate after Judgment Day and throughout eternity.

Heaven's inhabitants will include all of God's faithful, obedient, and righteous people throughout the ages who held to a shared hope, longing, and need for spiritual success in the kingdom of heaven. This is because the Scriptures reveal that, "Indeed, all who desire to live godly in Christ Jesus will be persecuted" (2 Timothy 3:12). The Greek word for persecuted, *dioko*, means mostly "to pursue (lit. or fig.); by [implication] to persecute: -- ensue, follow (after), given to, (suffer) persecute (ion), press toward." [2] This definition of persecution pertains to God's spiritually wounded warriors and Satan, with his demonic angels and human followers, are the persecutors. All manner of sin is the persecution they employ against God's people. Every person's physical and spiritual death is the desired result of Satan's plan using various forms of persecution and suffering.

Nevertheless, that same tyranny inspires God's devoted warriors to endure until life's end to attain their victory day! Subsequently, it is reasonable that Paul wrote the New Testament book of Ephesians to specifically instruct all Christians on protecting themselves from any satanic maltreatment. Persecutions regularly produce spiritually injured soldiers of Christ, at the least. Contrarywise, Paul's teachings here also enlighten and encourage spiritual warriors who are also constantly being made spiritually alive in Christ via His grace as the much better part (Ephesians 2:3-8). Of course, this also relies upon Christians maintaining their "unto-death" faithfulness (cf. Revelation 2:10). Every loyal warrior who continues their life-long devotion and achieves V-J Day is spiritually and eternally healthier.

Ephesians lists six ways Christians having "unto-death" devotion are continually made alive in Christ. In chapter *one*, faithful Christians are made alive in Christ by God's predetermined purpose or predestined will (verse 5). In chapter *two*, faithful Christians are made alive in Christ by God's divine favor or grace (verses 5, 8). In chapter *three*, faithful Christians are being made alive in Christ by the diversified wisdom or intelligence of God (Ephesians 3:10). In chapter *four*, faithful Christians are made alive in Christ by responding to the one call or invitation (ultimately to heaven) of God (verse 4). In chapter *five*, faithful Christians are made alive in Christ by being followers or imitators of God (verse 1). And in chapter *six*, faithful Christians are made alive in Christ by donning and keeping on the whole gospel armor (e.g., spiritual battle rattle) of God until death (verses 10-18).

In chapters four through six of Ephesians, Paul infers that Christians must do their part, whereas God performs His share in making us alive in Christ in chapters one through three. In the last part of chapter five and into chapter six, a Christian becomes an imitator or follower of God through obedience to Him. In the context of chapter six of Ephesians, compliance to God is the process of placing oneself in complete submission to all His commands. Whenever this happens, the saints (i.e., Christians made holy and set apart for a special purpose by the blood of Christ) having "unto-death" devotion are made alive in Christ by putting on the whole armor of God. The symbolic or divine battle gear worn by faithful Christian soldiers enables them to stand firm against satanic forces of evil and spiritual darkness (Ephesians 6:11,13). "Schemes" in this verse (Greek *methodia*) "denotes 'craft, deceit' ... 'wiles (of error).'" [3]

Paul implies that God enables faithful Christians to stand firm against Satan's schemes by wearing His entire armor, allowing them to minimize and recover from spiritual injuries incurred from his flaming missiles of temptation and sin. Paul was under house arrest for two years in Rome as he penned Ephesians, likely around A.D. 60-62. Guarded by reliable soldiers of the Roman Empire (Acts 28:16), he undoubtedly observed their battle dress of the time. Soldiers were appropriately attired to protect them against harm by their enemies in the event of a conflict. While surveying them, Paul wrote that Christians must also be outfitted in God's full battle rattle to protect their souls from Satan.

Whether faithfully attired in God's full gospel armor or not, all Christians who have fought Satan at one time or another are wounded warriors. In so doing, they have been spiritually hurt in the process, whether they know it or not. These soldiers have succumbed to battle wounds by no longer wearing the complete armor of God or maintaining their loyalty to Christ. Consequently, they may no longer desire spiritual triumph in obedience to the Scriptures. Conversely, their former fellow wounded warriors triumph over their battle injuries by maintaining their spiritual battle gear and lifetime faithfulness. The outcome is they continue to yearn for victory and remain steady in their obedient faith per the Scriptures. Therein lies the differences between *faithful* and *unfaithful* Christians or spiritual warriors, even when suffering battle wounds.

Therefore, from the book of Colossians, it seems that *faithful* spiritual soldiers understand that Christ is all they need to make them spiritually and eternally complete in heaven. In demonstrating that truth, Paul, from around A.D. 53-56, completed a three-year resident ministry in the historical city of Ephesus (Acts 20:31), situated in the Roman province of Asia Minor. He also spent two years teaching the gospel of Christ in the school of Tyrannus so that everyone living in the region heard about Him (Acts 19:9-10). One of those who obeyed the gospel was a man named Epaphras, who was a citizen of Colossae (located about one hundred miles east of Ephesus); he became a preacher and taught about Jesus in the churches at Colossae, Laodicea, and Hierapolis what he learned from Paul (Colossians 1:7; 4:12-13, 15-16).

Accordingly, the gospel (good news of Jesus Christ) spells out the hope of eternal life in heaven with Christ (Colossians 1:5; 3:3-4). This hope is for everyone who is made alive together with Christ through His forgiveness of their sins and transgressions (Colossians 1:14; 2:13). Once forgiven, those early Christians were further taught to keep living by faith in Christ just as they had received Him according to the gospel (Colossians 1:23; 2:6-7) and remain loyal to Him to realize the hope of eternal life in heaven with Jesus Christ. As beloved spiritually wounded warriors (Colossians 1:4), if any unfaithful soldier falls away and dies in their sins, they will forfeit all hope of realizing their day of triumph.

Previously, Paul and Epaphras' upholding obedience to the gospel of Christ as one's only hope of going to heaven (John 3:36; 2 Thessalonians 1:6-10; 1 Peter 4:17) encountered stiff resistance from oppositionists attempting to delude or deceive Christians by persuasive arguments. They did not yet have complete and accurate knowledge of the mystery of Christ (Colossians 2:1-4; Ephesians 3:4-6).

Having a convincing (Greek *pithanología*) argument means to impact others by using "persuasive speech, plausible discourse." [4] These self-seekers were altering the truth of the words or gospel of Christ as the Christians' only way to heaven (John 14:6). Consequently, they were trying to combine the Gentile philosophies (Colossians 2:8), Jewish celebrations (Colossians 2:16), and pagan rituals (Colossians 2:18, 23) of men as necessary to the practice of Christianity through false reasoning. In doing so, those supporting the integration of human ideals were trying to get resident Christians to seek worldly knowledge *plus* Christ seated in heaven at the right hand of God (Colossians 3:1).

If these syncretists (e.g., those who promote blending or merger) were successful in their endeavors, they would defraud Christian soldiers of their spiritual prize of eternal life (Colossians 2:18). Troubled over those set on depriving faithful Christians of their salvation, Epaphras apparently went to Rome sometime between A.D. 60-62 to inform Paul of this problem (Colossians 1:7-8). Under house arrest for preaching the gospel of Christ (Acts 28:30-31; Philippians 1:7; Philemon 13), Paul penned Colossians in answer to Epaphras' problem (Colossians 1:1; 4:16); he also wanted spiritually wounded soldiers to not miss out on their salvation. Paul also wrote the Colossians to encourage all Christians (Colossians 2:1-2; 4:8, 11). His encouragement was that one's hope of glory resides in a complete knowledge of the mystery of God that is Christ (Colossians 1:27; 2:2-3). This totality resides not in men's traditions or the elementary principles of the world as taught by the unionists (Colossians 2:8, 20). Nor does completeness live in matters that have the appearance of wisdom but have no value whatsoever (Colossians 2:23).

Jesus Christ is all one requires to make them complete and ready for spiritual and eternal life before physical death comes calling. Only then do spiritually wounded warriors who maintain an "unto-death" faithfulness throughout their lives in joyous awaiting and receipt of their victory. For all faithful Christian soldiers, including those spiritually wounded, the Bible reveals a progression or development from physical and temporal things to spiritual and eternal matters (Genesis 1:1, 26, 31; 2 Peter 3:8-13; Revelation 21:1-8).

First, the creation will advance when the old physical and temporal design is destroyed, giving way to the new spiritual and eternal plan. *Second*, people will grow as they move away from following unrighteousness to practicing righteousness through obedience to the gospel of Christ. *Third*, Christ, who made this progression the first time as a Man for salvation (Matthew 20:28), will return a second time in the clouds (Mark 14:62; 1 Thessalonians 4:16-18) to judge humanity (cf. Matthew 15:31; 1 Corinthians 4:5; 2 Corinthians 5:10). Any person failing to change before death or Jesus' second return will face His judgment and suffer eternal punishment (Matthew 25:46; 2 Thessalonians 1:9).

In conclusion, while all faithful Christian soldiers incur spiritual battle wounds in earth's physical (and temporal) realm, those injuries advance to complete healing and disappearance in heaven's spiritual and eternal kingdom. Why? Because they will come into Christ's presence, finally receiving their V-J Day medal—*Victory in Jesus* Day! (Far better than the Medal of Honor or any other earthly military award or citation.)

THOMAS WRIGHT, U.S. Air Force, Veteran
AFSC: Munitions Maintenance / Explosives Operator
EMAIL: tom-carla@juno.com

EDITOR'S NOTE: Tom holds a Bachelor of Theology, Master of Biblical Studies, and a Doctor of Ministry degree.

ENDNOTES:

1 Joe D. Jones, *Victory in Jesus: A Study of the Book of Revelation*. (Searcy, AR:

Joe D. Jones, 1990), 50.

2 James Strong, *The New Strong's Complete Dictionary of Bible Words*. (Nashville: Thomas Nelson Publishers, 1996), 605.

3 W. E. Vine, *Schemes. Vine's Complete Expository Dictionary of Old and New Testament Words: With Topical Index*. (Nashville: Thomas Nelson Publishers, 1996), 676.

4 Wesley J. Perschbacher, ed. *The New Analytical Greek Lexicon*. (Peabody, MA: Hendrickson Publishers, Inc., 1990), 327.

5 T.G. Wright, *Satan: The Persecuting Prosecutor of God and His People*. (Colorado Springs, CO: Private Label Publishing, 2012), 57.

EPILOGUE
The Sum of All Tears

If you have read this book and got to this point (unless you are one of those who flip to the end to see what is there), then you have been on a unique mission. The book's title or something you read early on caught your interest, and you kept going. Or, maybe, you were desperately searching for some answers to your spiritual wounding(s).

We have discussed some pretty severe and spiritually life-threatening stuff here, including battle injuries, missing in action, dying, suicide, and how to address those. Perhaps you have gained some insight and practical ways of managing and dressing your wounds. But, even most important than all, what you should walk away from reading this book is *hope*. That is what you and I need most.

You don't have to know me very long to find out I am a big superhero nerd. Marvel, DC, I am no respecter of heroes. I like 'em all—been reading comics since I was old enough to read. I remember being able to buy three comics wrapped in cellophane, with the covers torn off, not knowing what the middle one was until you opened the package—all for 19 cents. I thought that having some kind of super-powers would be the ultimate. Yes, I was that kid running around the house with a bath towel for a cape, saving the day and rescuing those who needed help.

Some time ago, a dad had asked his son what superpower he would choose if he could. His son thought for a moment and then said, "I would want the power to not ever have to go pee." His dad said, "What? Of all the powers available, you want the power to be able to hold your bladder?" The son said, "Yeah, Dad. Think of all the time I could save. I would never have to stop playing to go inside and pee." His dad replied, "Son, I think that is the lamest superpower I've ever heard of. What is your name going to be? No-Pee man? Super Bladder Dude? You've got to come up with something better than that!" I was dying of laughter.

Who would not want to have some type of superpower? More to the point, to control something we do not have control over. But really, underneath all that is the yearning for hope. Hope is the fuel for all other possibilities. If you can dream it, you can pursue it passionately. Incidentally, people who have lost hope often say, "I just feel so powerless." There are two types of hope. One is hoping for *something*, and the other is hoping for *someone*. Hoping for something to happen, change, be different, transform, go away or even come back will eventually disappoint us. Every circumstance, every situation, and every relationship we put our hope in will wear out, give out, fall apart, meltdown, or go away at some point. The only hope that will last is hope in someone.

The following is a long passage, but it is essential to our understanding of hope. Hang with me and read it to the end:

> Moses said to GOD, 'Look, you tell me, 'Lead this people,' but you don't let me know whom you're going to send with me. You tell me, 'I know you well and you are special to me.' If I am so special to you, let me in on your plans. That way, I will continue being special to you. Don't forget, this is your people, your responsibility.' GOD said, 'My presence will go with you. I'll see the journey to the end.' Moses said, 'If your presence doesn't take the lead here, call this trip off right now. How else will it be known that you're with me in this, with me and your people? Are you traveling with us or not? How else will we know that we're special, I and your people, among all other people on this planet earth?' GOD said to Moses: 'All right. Just as you say; this also I will do, for I know you well and you are special to me. I know you by name.' (Exodus 33:12-17, MSG)

That was Moses' superpower—God's very presence! The Super Power that trumped all others. Did Moses have hope? You bet he did— how could he not? Every step of the way to the land of Canaan, God (*God* mind you!) was right there, leading by day and night, providing food, shelter, water, and safety.

We have that same hope. Jesus, Immanuel, God with us. Does He know you by name? Does He see your struggle(s), your wounding(s)?

Yes, He does. This hope will see you through your battle injuries and on your way to something brighter and better. Hold on to hope; it will not disappoint or put you to shame (Romans 5:5).

DARREN CROWDEN, U.S. Air Force, Retired
EMAIL: cnerrad@yahoo.com

FINAL NOTE

Spiritual wounds can result from mental health issues arising from various causes, often requiring professional care. If you, a loved one, or a friend is struggling with physical or emotional abuse, or other problems, seek help by contacting your installation or unit chaplain, minister, or another qualified professional. If you are having thoughts of suicide, call **911** or **988** (the new Veterans Suicide and Crisis Lifeline effective July 16, 2022). "'During a crisis, every second counts,' said VA Secretary Denis McDonough. 'This new, shorter number makes it easier for Veterans and those who care about them to reach lifesaving support without having to be enrolled in VA benefits or health care.'"[1]

Do not isolate yourself but lean on your spiritual battle buddy and church family who will love and pray for you. Above all, continue to pray to and seek divine help from the Great Physician who can heal your body, mind, and soul. *Shalom.*

ENDNOTE:

1 *Crisis Line.* https://www.va.gov/connecticut-health-care/stories/dial-988-new-veterans-crisis-line-phone-number/

EXHIBIT A

Military Jargon / Acronyms

AIT	Advanced Individual Training (Army)
AFSC	Air Force Specialty Code
AWOL	Absent Without Leave
FORSCOM	Forces Command (Army)
IED	Improvised Explosive Device
KIA	Killed In Action
MEDDAC	Medical Department Activity (Army)
MILMIN	Military Ministry
MOS	Military Occupational Specialty (Army)
MRE	Meal, Ready-To-Eat
NCOIC	Noncommissioned Officer in Charge
OCONUS	Outside Contiguous United States
PCS	Permanent Change of Station
POW	Prisoner of War
PTSD	Post-Traumatic Stress Disorder
RATING	Navy Enlisted Jobs
ROTC	Reserve Officer Training Corps
RPG	Rocket-Propelled Grenade
R & R	Rest and Recuperation
TDY	Temporary Duty
QRF	Quick Reaction Force
UCMJ	Uniformed Code of Military Justice

EXHIBIT B
Bible Translations / Versions

HCSB Holman Christian Standard Bible
MSG   The Message
NASB New American Standard Bible
NIV   New International Version
NLT   New Living Translation

Made in the USA
Columbia, SC
28 April 2025